M000074485

BRAVE TEACHING

Bringing Emotional-Resiliency Skills
from the Wilderness to the Classroom

Krissy Pozatek, MSW
and Sarah Love, MA

LANTERN BOOKS / NEW YORK
A Division of Booklight, Inc.

Krissy:
FOR JASMINE AND AMELIE
my inspirations to be a better person every day

Sarah:
FOR YOU, MOM

CONTENTS

INTERNAL-RESILIENCY SKILLS

Problem-Solving

Adaptability

Emotional Regulation

Ownership of Emotions and Behaviors

Assertive Communication

Perspective Taking

Delayed Gratification

Reframing Struggle

Sitting with Discomfort

Mindfulness

Executive Functioning and Organization

If you read through this list, you'll notice how young people lack these skills today. *Brave Teaching* shows teachers how to develop them in students.

FOREWORD

THIS BOOK IS a collaboration between me, Krissy Pozatek, a former wilderness therapist and current parent coach, and Sarah Love, a fourth-grade teacher. Sarah integrated the concepts she found in my book *Brave Parenting* into her own parenting and then into her classroom and school. Sarah saw emotional growth in her son and students that was so significant and so easy to implement that she couldn't keep quiet about it. She saw her students take ownership of their emotions and accountability for their behaviors, and self-regulate, problem-solve, and achieve a maturity unimaginable to her based on her previous years' teaching. *Brave Parenting* provided the material that Sarah was seeking and not finding in the classroom-management books and training she'd received as a teacher.

The aim of *Brave Teaching* is to take into teaching the emotional-growth concepts that I transferred from wilderness therapy into parenting and wrote about in *Brave Parenting*. Students need to learn these precious life skills at all ages of development. Self-regulation and emotional maturation need to be brought from therapy offices and therapy programs into schools and homes to benefit all kids/students. The aim of education is not only to expand students' intellects, but also to equip them with internal resiliency so they can get where they need to go in life. Thank you, teachers, for taking this journey to become "brave teachers."

Note: This book is intended for students from kindergarten to twelfth grade. Although Sarah reflects on working with her son in first and second grades, and with her fourth-grade class, my primary experience is with preteens to young adults (from ages eleven to twenty). All the concepts in this book will be shown to be adaptable to the different grade levels, specifically in Part 2. The material is transferrable to all age groups, even adults!

All of the stories in this book mirror accounts of interactions between students and teachers told to the authors of this book. Although the themes are congruent, details within each vignette have been fictionalized for teaching purposes and to protect identities.

INTRODUCTION

Sarah Love and Krissy Pozatek

🌿 **SARAH WRITES:** I believe that all parents want what is best for their kids. For me, this dream started the moment I became pregnant. I imagined how my life would go as a parent, how I would raise my son, and the success he would achieve, and even the moments he would attribute his greatness and accomplishments to me. I felt that parenting would come naturally, and that my child and I would form a close relationship; I did not anticipate any hardships. This plan, however, fell apart as soon as he was born. Parenting is humbling, and I went from a place of confidence about being a parent to doubting everything I was doing. Why was this? Because of the newfound love I had for my son, I began to forget about raising him and instead rescued him at every moment. I was scared of doing something wrong as a parent and worked hard to avoid every potential struggle, discomfort, or problem that might impact him.

My journey as a parent has been filled with great intensity, love, fear, joy, pain, and self-doubt. When my son was six months old, his father and I split because we were moving in different directions and a path together was not in our future. I immediately felt so much guilt that I was going to raise my son in a split home that I began to respond to every one of his needs so he didn't feel ripped off. Thus, our enmeshment began: I worked hard to guard his feelings, and he fulfilled my loneliness, and we became one unit. It was he and I against the world. I protected, rescued, and provided for him. I received compliments from many people, and believed I was the best single mother in the world.

As my son grew older, I felt more out of control. When he was emotional, I thought I wasn't giving him enough of what he needed, and in turn reacted emotionally myself. When my son got into grade school, he began attending the school where I taught. I thought this would be the best outcome for both of us; unfortunately, it enmeshed us even more. My emotional pain increased because all I wanted to do was fix every hard thing he had to go through. In first grade, he began to get into a bit of trouble and seemed to lack self-regulation.

At this point, my self-doubt became acute: What had I done wrong? Was my son acting out because of the decisions I'd made as a parent? How could I sort this out so it would all just go away? I did what most parents would do: I began blaming everyone else for his decisions and tried to control his environment even more. Although my plan worked for a brief period, they were only quick fixes. My son's behavior seemed to worsen.

The summer after my son's first grade, I watched as he had constant emotional meltdowns, anxiety, and couldn't even brush his teeth without me standing next to him. I had raised an anxious, codependent child, and I was stuck as a parent.

I was desperate for help and came across *Brave Parenting*. In her book, Krissy focuses on raising emotionally resilient kids and—boy!— did I need that! Krissy's philosophy is that we parents must let our children sit with their emotions, allow them to feel, and then teach them how to develop their own problem-solving skills. Her philosophy encouraged me to be brave enough to let my son begin to handle decisions on his own and take ownership of them. I started out small, merely validating his emotions and letting him feel them instead of trying to fix them. When he had an emotional meltdown, my response every time was, "I can see you're upset. When you want to talk about it, I will be ready."

Though these sentences seem simple, they were extremely powerful. They validated my son's feelings and created a safe space in which he could be upset. I began to see change almost immediately. After many weeks of using this response, I added boundaries when he had meltdowns: "I can see you're upset. It's OK to be upset. But it's not OK to behave that way. When you're ready, I'll talk to you about it." Believe it or not, self-regulation develops quickly when the parent doesn't rescue a child, and he or she has to do it on his or her own.

By the end of the summer, my son was completely different. As he entered second grade, he was more independent. He was no longer anxious and didn't expect me to be with him all the time. He trusted himself. My son, who in first grade couldn't even complete a class assignment and cried about doing any schoolwork at home, completed class assignments and was responsible for his homework at home, and his meltdowns had almost entirely ended.

I thought that if this could work with my son, I might be able to bring these techniques to school—to teach children how to be independent problem-solvers and develop emotional resiliency in the classroom.

TEACHING

Teachers encounter all sorts of stress. We're expected to close the gap on academics, achieve excellent test scores, and be highly effective—all the while teaching kids how to make good decisions and please their parents. It's not an easy job. When I decided to use Krissy's philosophy in my classroom, I promised myself I'd let go of stressors as a teacher and implement it fully. It was hard at the beginning. I was very worried about losing control. Many of us who rescue kids (parents, teachers, and coaches) might think we're being empathic, but really we seek control. I realized this when I tried to give up rescuing. I worried that, if my approach failed, my students would be negatively affected. Would I upset parents with the new routine in my classroom? What if it backfired and produced worse results? I had to consider all of these questions before I could let go.

My classroom consisted of twenty-two students, nine of whom received some type of services from the school. I have been a teacher for many years and have taught many ages, including special needs, as well as private behavior therapy. I believe myself to be adept when it comes to behavior, and I'm a big advocate of reinforcement. Though I didn't struggle with classroom management, I *did* when it came to teaching children to become independent thinkers and be emotionally resilient.

The goal of this book is to help teachers not just have compliant students, but students who are respectful, accountable, and independent—which is why I take the issue of control and teacher authority so seriously. Honestly, my first year as a teacher was awful. College didn't prepare me for the challenges I faced. I had thirty-five full-day kindergarten students; only five of them spoke English. I genuinely didn't know what I was doing or where to begin when it came to managing my students. I had only minimal knowledge of classroom management, and the results were disastrous: I had no authority and my kids ran the show. I went home every night exhausted and in tears. I'm sure I was not alone; many teachers can relate to that exact experience. Though many of us over time develop the skills we need to run a smooth classroom, we still encounter problems with students. Even if we're experienced and able teachers, with excellent management abilities, we still have students who seem only to be successful when they're with us.

Like many teachers and parents today, I've been guilty of emotional rescuing. I'm very attuned to people's behavior and see cues in children's stress levels. I was constantly on alert, managing emotions. I tended to swoop in and change the environment in order for these students to complete their tasks, and it's fair to say I did this with *all* my students. (This strategy also helped make learning relatively stress-free.) I had absorbed the mentality that success in the classroom will equal future achievement and a happy life. And my students *were* very successful— but only with my external management.

I spent a lot of time, especially after recess, dealing with "issues." All teachers can attest to the reality that, when we're not around, the students seem to fall apart, and we're left with hours of managing them to get the students back on track. Wouldn't it be nice to create a classroom of students who take responsibility for their own choices and can problem-solve on their own? I noticed as a teacher that not only was I fixing every issue, I was also frustrated when the problems continued and even worsened. Even when I talked, preached, and taught kids how to behave in the classroom, the lessons seemed to disappear once they moved on to a space without me. I quickly learned that because I was solving every issue (even those with parents), I was creating dependency. I realized when reading *Brave Parenting* that in fixing students' problems, I was placing their problems on my lap; I was making their problems my own and working hard to find their solution. In my efforts to "help," I was undermining students' abilities to take ownership and learn how to solve difficulties themselves.

This reality doesn't end with students. When teachers receive an email from a dissatisfied parent, we tend to react immediately with a quick fix so tension with parents can de-escalate and they're not unhappy with us. But what if responding that way is really what keeps parents upset and even gives them an opportunity to blame you if things don't go the way they want? In my experience, the quick fix can lead to teachers being blamed rather than identifying how children can be accountable and responsible for their behavior. These were the conditions I was hoping to change by implementing *Brave Parenting* in my classroom with students and parents.

IMPLEMENTING **BRAVE PARENTING**

In order to perfect my craft I had to let go of my control/fixing/dependency patterns. After all, I'd been owning not only my students' problems, but their successes, too. As students continued on to other teachers and schools, I knew they'd not have teachers to tweak their environments to make them successful. I now know that this external management provides temporary rescue and a feeling of success, but it doesn't build a child's self-regulation skills. I needed to foster their independence and emotional maturation so they could be successful regardless of the teacher or school, because the success was internal.

I had to create an environment safe enough to allow kids to genuinely struggle. This was painful, even for me as a teacher. Our society doesn't like discomfort. We neither want to watch kids in distress nor allow them to remain so without intervening. How many times have we presented a student with a math problem, seen them become frustrated because they could not solve it immediately, and stepped in so they didn't have to feel uncomfortable? Schools have become aware of this pattern and developed a new practice of the growth mindset, which allows kids to make mistakes. The only hitch is that no one ever taught us teachers how to help our students *emotionally* manage the struggle so they would develop the skills to endure through mistakes.

Encouraging students to stick with a problem even when it's hard, and reframing that struggle as success from failure, is a great concept. But what if kids can't manage the emotional side of that concept? We assume that if we give our students opportunities to fail or find things difficult then they'll grow stronger. But this may not be the case. Many families don't allow struggle at home; helicopter parenting rescues kids from challenge and difficulty. So if kids don't possess the ability to cope with discomfort, simply letting them struggle or fail may not be helpful at all.

This is a skills gap—meaning what we expect of children is beyond their ability to handle it. This gap can lead to what all teachers see: misbehavior, disrespect, shutting down, and students turning elsewhere to self-medicate. We can tell our students not to become upset and stay strong, to discover their mistakes and get better, but is it really that easy? Do we tell a child who has never held a pencil simply to start writing? No. We have to teach them *how* to hold the pencil. *What is missing is emotional-skills development: for students to identify, feel, and process feelings; for students to learn to be with their own discomfort.* Emotional attunement teaches kids that it is safe to sit with their feelings and feel. Just as in teaching a child to hold a pencil, you have to start with the basics. When kids learn that it's safe to experience their feelings without reactivity, they become able to manage the emotions that come up around struggle. First A and then B.

For instance, I had a student who completely shut down if she couldn't find the answer immediately. It was exhausting for both of us. I was a firm believer in the growth mindset and in letting her wrestle with the difficulty. But she didn't know how to struggle through, so it was a continuous challenge as I encouraged her to grapple with the issue and reminded her that failure was OK. There was no growth. After many days of nothing changing, I realized she couldn't get through the difficulty emotionally. She did not have this skill.

I decided to change my focus, using what I was learning in *Brave Parenting*, and asked her to problem-solve the struggle (the emotions), and not the math. I asked her what she was feeling and if she was fine with sitting with that emotion, even if it caused her distress. I told her that discomfort was a normal and safe emotion to feel. I encouraged her to use a breathing technique she had learned in our "calm classroom" curriculum. I also allowed her to ask for advice if she wanted. After focusing on the process, I finally began to see growth. Instead of rescuing, I reframed the struggle and gave her opportunities to ask for help, find a solution, and remain uncomfortable. The growth mindset is powerful, and this book will help you learn how to close the emotional-skills gap and use it successfully with your students.

As I implemented *Brave Parenting* philosophies in my classroom, I made it clear to students that they were responsible for themselves and were required to take ownership of everything: their emotions, behavior, and schoolwork, or lack thereof. I also affirmed that everything was a choice within the boundaries and expectations of the classroom. I call them "classroom agreements." The students are first and foremost responsible for owning and regulating their feelings and solving their problems (with support available). They are answerable for their schoolwork and their behavior in the classroom. Different measures in the classroom structure help to keep the students accountable to these classroom agreements. I use the language of choice, which is a formidable disrupter of power struggles.

For example, students can decide whether to hand in their homework on time or not. If they don't, they are choosing behaviors outside of the classroom agreements and face the corresponding consequence, such as attending study-lunch. They also have a choice with their emotions: for example, whether to stay angry or not. Framing emotions as a choice is extremely empowering, for kids and adults alike. I don't tell students how to feel. I don't cheer them up or rush them out of feelings; their emotions are theirs to experience—just as their problems are theirs to problem-solve, and not for someone else to fix. This framework disrupts any blame and emotional manipulation and quickly changes the attitude of all students in my class.

One of my students (let's call her Diane) struggled daily with control. If Diane wasn't in control, she was unhappy and likely to melt down. In my class, the line leader is expected to stand in a certain spot, and the rest of the kids follow. In this case, the line leader was in the correct location, and Diane was behind the line leader. One of the other children was too close to the line leader's spot, creating a bunching effect. The line was shifting forward. Diane grew frustrated and started arguing with another girl in class, insisting that she move. When I came over and responded with "It seems there is a disagreement," Diane impulsively reacted with "SHE WON'T MOVE!" I reminded Diane that she was responsible for her feelings and for finding a solution. I asked her if she'd like to talk about it.

As we discussed ownership of emotions, Diane realized that she was the one getting upset. Because she was unable to control her peers and the choices they made, she could only control her own choices and behaviors. Diane resolved that next time *she* would move to a new spot. At this point, Diane couldn't blame me for taking sides or trying to fix the problem. She realized on her own that it was *her* emotion that caused the situation to escalate, resulting in confrontation with another classmate. Diane recognized that she had a choice to remain angry or let it go. She chose the latter and was able to get back on track quickly.

It's amazing to see the change in motivation when you're given options. Whether you're a student or teacher, a visible and felt sense of relief washes over you when you have a choice, as well as the empowerment that comes from knowing you're in control of that choice. The opposite plays out regularly in classrooms, where students feel powerless and perceive themselves as victims of the situation and then resort to blame. I learned as a teacher that all those moments I used to see as frustrating were opportunities to help my students build resilience. I became less internally reactive and more accepting of all the "issues" that arose every day. I didn't externally manage anymore. I didn't swoop in and fix. I allowed things to fall apart and asked kids to use their skills to respond appropriately.

This process is by no means a magic formula that happens in one day and your student will never have another bad day or a meltdown. However, these tools create a healthy learning environment where kids are encouraged to feel all their emotions and learn to regulate the behaviors that follow as a result.

REINFORCING CONCEPTS

In building this classroom culture, I have had to keep reinforcing these concepts. At the beginning of the year, we read many books about the growth mindset, as well as problems we encounter in life, at school, and with emotions. Every time we read a book, we discuss connections with the book and whether we've had a similar experience. This self-application helps expand background knowledge, which is crucial in forming a deeper connection to what we're learning. We then make a class promise (classroom agreement) and develop accountability measures that will be used if a student chooses to break our classroom promises (the norms we establish).

The next part of the process is deciding how I, as a teacher, will respond to a student when a promise is broken or when emotions arise and issues follow. Teachers need to develop the skill of letting go as well. We must learn not to take something personally. Our students will struggle and explode, and we must be their guide through that emotion instead of being reactive or fixing it. When situations have occurred in my classroom, my response has been similar to the one I used with my son. That response stays consistent in every situation, and I don't change it based on a different student. I employ this consistency because I don't want any students to feel as if I'm choosing sides or treating individuals differently. This attitude is vital if you want to develop independent learners, because students must respect you if you want to see change. If you're shifting what you say and altering accountability measures for different children, they'll notice it.

The response I used for students who were clearly undergoing some kind of emotion was, "I can see that you are [emotion]. Would you like to talk about it?" If a student broke a classroom promise, I would add, "It appears you are [poor choice] in our classroom. We do not [behave this way]. Because you chose to [poor choice], your accountability measure is [consequence]."

It's important to use language that creates a sense of belonging. Using *my* classroom, *my* rules, and *my* expectations only fosters an absence of ownership. Students will feel like this is *your* environment and they must obey, rather than feeling they are part of something and are responsible for every decision they make. Thus, we employ *our* classroom, *our* rules, and *our* expectations when addressing any issues. The more you use such language, the more you take away your emotional response when a child has made a poor choice or is emotional.

Once again, this change doesn't happen overnight. However, the transition from dependent, emotional students to independent emotional regulators can occur fairly rapidly. This is not surprising. When you have no one to rescue you, you respond quickly. If you are consistent, students will begin to rely on their own skills rather than always needing you to fix a problem. Even students who are rescued at home will still respond if you remain consistent. You may even see a change in their home environment. Most kids want to feel in control of themselves, and this technique allows for the opportunity—if you let them.

One feature of *Brave Parenting* that resonated with me is Krissy's observation that a quick fix is like pressing the repeat button. We reinforce the same dynamics that play out day after day with the same challenging students who want control, or the same hyperactive students disrupting the class, and so on. They are passively waiting to be managed externally. But as parents and teachers, we always have a choice: we can rescue again today or hold students accountable to foster skills for tomorrow. We can use every scenario as an opportunity to build internal self-regulation, accountability, and emotional growth, such as I learned with the situations above.

Another burden of helicopter parenting that has fallen hard on teachers is the high prevalence of issues regarding executive functioning. Whether a child has been diagnosed with attention-deficit disorder (ADD) or not, many parents remind, organize, and manage their children, so they aren't learning to complete these executive functions themselves. Teachers are therefore left to accommodate these skill deficits in children. We can either continue to externally manage or try to build these internal-resiliency skills in the classroom.

One of my students this year (we'll call him Noah) was diagnosed with attention-deficit/hyperactivity disorder (ADHD) and had major problems with executive functions. He struggled with writing down homework, and inevitably at four o'clock in the afternoon every day, I'd receive an email from Noah's mother (whom we'll call Carol) asking what Noah's homework was, because he'd forgotten to write it down. Because she came from a good place and always helped her son, Carol would then ask me to email her Noah's homework. I understand this helped Carol hold Noah accountable at home. But how on earth was this supposed to enable Noah to become independent enough to write down his homework? Initially, I tried reminding Noah at the end of the day to complete this task. But if you are familiar with executive-functioning issues, you'll know that organization, reminders, and creating lists are a challenge. I needed to come up with a plan—one that helped Noah execute the task and hold him accountable if he didn't.

Noah was to set the reoccurring alarm on his iPad every day for three o'clock to a specific noise that applied only to him writing down his homework. Then when the alarm went off, he'd immediately write his homework down. He didn't have to check in with me, because the task was his responsibility. If he failed to do it, then he'd not be able to complete his homework (I stopped emailing Carol) and I would hold him accountable. We discussed the accountability measure together, and Noah decided that if he didn't write down his homework, he'd have to complete all outstanding homework during "Fun Friday."

In the beginning, Carol was nervous and didn't buy into the plan. She feared, not unreasonably, that Noah would spend all his Fun Friday on homework, because he struggled to write it down. Nonetheless, if Noah was ever going to learn this responsibility, he had to get uncomfortable and not be rescued. And Noah *was* uncomfortable, and he *did* struggle a lot. But he also learned that he had a choice either to continue forgetting to write his homework down and miss Fun Friday or to respond to the alarm and immediately write it down. With this choice, Noah eventually changed his behavior. When that alarm went off, he dropped everything and wrote down his homework consistently. Noah was uncomfortable enough with the accountability measure and eventually learned that no one was there to rescue him. So he changed.

In today's society, kids receive many accommodations: some warranted and some perhaps created out of fear. Nevertheless, we're seeing a major increase in children with some kind of disability or impairment. Though, legally, we need to honor these accommodations, we can still hold kids accountable and improve self-regulation skills in students. The issue is not the accommodations, but creating enough uncomfortableness that self-regulation naturally appears. How many times do we change our behavior when we're comfortable? Not many. This is why accountability and ownership are so important and will work even if other factors are at play, such as a disability.

———

WHEN I FIRST began adapting *Brave Parenting*, I wondered whether teachers could maintain teacher authority with any type of classroom. Could teachers actually educate students in emotional resiliency and self-regulation? Could we have a challenging classroom and still allow safe struggle? Could kids who were more troublesome still learn these skills? In college, many of us were not fully trained on successful classroom management. We didn't learn properly how to teach problem-solving, emotional self-regulation, or how to work with parents. Additionally, many teachers have experienced an upset parent, and, without realizing it, we try to fix what the parent is feeling, and this frequently results in blaming the teacher. Learning the skills to work effectively with students and respond to parents appropriately will help take the blame off of teachers and create a healthy working relationship between teacher and parent. If we don't know or understand these concepts, teaching can be very challenging.

I want to encourage all teachers to take on a new journey with your classroom, to be a "brave teacher." We can accomplish these goals with the emotional skills taught in *Brave Teaching*. ❧

KRISSY WRITES: Sarah reached out to me after she began implementing *Brave Parenting* concepts in her classroom and school. I don't know that every person can read a parenting book and apply the concepts within a different setting (in this case a classroom) so adeptly and proficiently. But after meeting Sarah, I saw she possessed a high emotional literacy and a readiness for this type of material. Sarah wanted a curriculum that fostered not just a student's intellect, but also his or her emotional skills and ability to be successful. Sarah wanted a way to promote a student's maturation, ownership, and accountability, and to teach skills such as emotion-regulation, problem-solving, and self-awareness, not to mention executive functioning. I am not a teacher, nor am I fluent in the trainings and curricula teachers have at their disposal. But after hearing from Sarah, it became evident to me that the classroom could be a learning container to promote these skills, just like a home environment.

Brave Teaching educates teachers on how to bring these "essential ingredients" into the classroom. Part 1 explains the four essential ingredients, and Part 2 introduces specific exercises to further these concepts and skills in your students.

First, I need to tell you my background and where I learned concepts around processing emotions and emotional resiliency. There follows a brief introduction to wilderness therapy.

chapter 1

WHERE I LEARNED IT ALL

Wilderness Therapy

MEET BEN: A dirty, fourteen-year-old kid sitting in dusty red sand in the middle of a Utah desert. Next to him is his backpack and a shelter he made out of tarp, string, and rocks he found around this site. At this point, Ben has already logged forty days in the wilderness, and during his morning break he's whittled a stick into a spoon. As he does so, he's aware of the sensory environment around him. He notices the grain of the wood in his hand. He listens to the other group members and hears the birds flit about in the trees above. He feels the warmth of the sun on his beanie, and he smells the remains of the smoke of last night's fire in the coal pit. All the while, he stays focused on his knife's movement. He observes his breath moving in and out. He senses calmness in his body and peace in his mind. He has found the present moment. He is content.

It hasn't always been this way. Ben's family chose a "wilderness intervention" after a period of thirteen months where Ben was spiraling downward at home. This same satisfied boy one month previously refused to go to school; he was anxious and depressed, and he isolated himself in his room. He smoked cigarettes when he could and played or thought about video games most hours of the day—to the degree that professionals mentioned the term *gaming addiction* applied to him. He preferred Xbox and social media to interacting socially.

It was clear Ben felt trapped. He was not happy. His mother was always telling him what to do, so he yelled at her. His father was always getting angry, so he avoided him. When he did talk to his parents, the conversation usually turned into another battle or power struggle. He also lied and was usually defiant about their rules. Ben had also disconnected from most of his engagements: sports, school, family, even friends. After two months of Ben not going to school and lots of office therapy that didn't amount to much, Ben's parents were at their wits' end. They decided to try another solution.

Ben hated the wilderness at first. He spent the initial two weeks blaming his parents for all his problems. He wanted to be at home and to sleep in his bed and have all his electronics. He wanted a fridge full of food, hot showers, and his music. He wanted his friends, his social media accounts, and his clothes, not to mention his freedom. Contrast this Ben with the boy whittling the spoon. The latter doesn't have anything that is *his* in a material sense; all his clothing, gear, and food is issued by the program. Yet, without all the distractions, this Ben has something he never found at home: peace of mind. The wilderness experience has given him an opportunity to reflect and be with his thoughts and his feelings.

Because "wilderness Ben" didn't have anything he wanted or thought he needed, he had to adjust. This internal adjustment is called maturation. When kids accept their external reality and learn to self-manage their internal reality, they mature.

I should note that Ben actually found wilderness therapy a welcome change, as most students do. In addition to learning how to hike with a heavy backpack, make a primitive bow-drill fire, do camp chores, and sleep under a tarp, Ben discovered that all his feelings were OK—even if he was anxious, angry, or depressed. The field staff and counselors listened calmly and validated all his emotions. They nodded, created space for his feelings, and kept listening. No one rushed him out of his emotions, told him how to feel, or tried to cheer him up or fix his problems. No adults lectured him or rationalized about what he "should" be doing.

What Ben learned is that feelings weren't the problem: his behavior was. If Ben was angry, that was OK. If Ben yelled, acted disrespectfully, or was defiant, then he'd be held accountable. This was a challenge at first. Ben was used to escalating his emotions to get his way. But it didn't work here; Ben discovered that adults simply listened to his feelings. However, if his feelings turned into unacceptable behavior, then he was held accountable, which most likely led to losing privileges.

Ben found the distinction between his emotions and behavior refreshing. In fact, wilderness therapy teaches that *underneath all behavior is a feeling*. This is why wilderness therapy places so much value and emphasis on identifying, owning, and sharing feelings. When kids talk about their feelings they are *much* less likely to act them out with a behavior. Ben learned that if he felt anxious, he could talk about it *or* act it out. He always had a choice. If he shut down and refused to participate, or if he was rude and snapped at others, these behaviors would usually lead to some accountability measure: group feedback, a loss of trust in the group, or something more specific like forgoing the privilege of using the camp chair, or less social time with the group.

Ben noticed that even the consequences were different from home. When he was held accountable by the program there was no tone of emotion or judgment that he was bad or disappointing his parents, as he'd received at home. This, too, was refreshing. He simply lost a privilege that day, and he noticed that he didn't like *any* infringement on his privileges, even if it was as apparently insignificant as social time by the fire or a camp chair.

Instead, Ben received the message every day that experiencing difficulty is normal, OK, and even beneficial. This was a *big* shift for him. Ben was used to acting helpless in the face of a struggle and giving up, even while he secretly wanted his parents, friends, or teachers to rescue him. His act usually worked. Not here. In the wilderness, struggle is framed as an essential part of life, not something to tamper with. If

Ben found things hard, the staff and counselors let him. They were patient, compassionate, supportive, and at times firm if he acted out. But they never rescued him, unless safety necessitated helping him complete a chore before a lightning storm came. Although challenging situations annoyed Ben at first, he grew to like them. He could no longer manipulate others to do things for him, so he stopped putting energy into these old behaviors. He felt capable, empowered, and much more resilient when he knew that the only way to do something was to do it himself.

Ben had never genuinely understood accountability before. Now he saw it as a powerful way to own his behavior and choices. Ben also had a choice in every moment around his emotions: to talk about them or act them out. These self-management skills helped Ben increase his self-awareness, which in turn translated into more self-esteem and confidence. This led to a greater empowerment to own his own life. What a contrast with his previous strategy of "life-avoidance"!

The staff routinely took pictures of Ben and the other group members to send to his parents, who were heartened to see light had returned to their son's eyes. Although he was pretty dirty, he had a genuine smile, and looked happy in a way he hadn't since he was little. Ben's parents were overjoyed that their lost child seemed to have returned. They realized that he'd created the happiness himself; he'd made a choice to engage in the program. However, although Ben's parents were pleased about his progress, uncertainty still loomed about how to proceed after wilderness.

MY JOURNEY INTO THE WILDERNESS

Immediately after graduating from college, I drove to Utah and began working as a field instructor in a wilderness-therapy program. I found the work exhilarating and all-encompassing. We undertook week-long shifts with struggling teens from all over the United States, and beyond. As I adjusted to a primitive life—falling asleep under the stars;

cooking on a fire; and setting up my shelter each night by cotton-woods, junipers, sage, and aspens—I acclimated to the rhythms of the high desert: its smells, sunrises, and sunsets. Nature's calm seeped into me, and I felt more present and alive. I became much more alert and aware of the world around me. I learned the names of plants, animals, constellations, and weather patterns. Although I looked forward to beds with sheets, hot showers, and refrigerated foods, and at times I was greatly challenged by the kids, I found a peace I'd not known in my previous, indoor life.

In order to continue this work, I went to graduate school and returned as a therapist to keep connecting to and enhancing my skills with kids. My new role led me to work much more closely with the parents of the children in the program. In addition to weekly individual sessions and groups with the kids in the woods, I now spent two days a week in my office on the phone with parents, conducting family therapy. I also led day-long seminars when the parents came to visit. This activity exposed me much more to the struggles on the other end of the child–parent equation. I learned what these kids were like at home and how caught and stuck the parents felt because of their children's struggles. I worked with the parents in the most effective way I could.

I became a mother, and my husband and I decided to move from Utah to the East Coast and closer to family. It was suggested to me that I work with parents. I was intrigued as it was always disheartening to see kids make tremendous progress in programs only to have that progress reversed when they returned home. In 2006, I started my parent-coaching business, Parallel Process, LLC. Initially, it was an adjustment, as I'd been so focused on the child for so many years. Yet as I became more skilled, I felt grateful to work with parents, as I believe the ability for each child to retain the gains of treatment programs rests largely on how well the home supports these changes.

In making my shift toward helping parents, I identified what I call the "essential ingredients" of wilderness therapy that help create emotional growth and internal resiliency. I identified wilderness as the "learning container." The main goal of my parent coaching was to bring these ingredients into everyday parenting. I knew what naturally happened in the wilderness setting because of behavioral boundaries and emotional attunement. Was it possible to build these internal skills in the home? Could any parent promote their children's maturation, even if a child didn't do a wilderness intervention? Might parents of younger children sidestep delays in pre-adolescent and adolescent maturation and keep kids' emotional development on track? My answer to all three questions was, and is, an unequivocal *Yes!*

If parents can make the home a learning container, with the four essential ingredients, I believe they can create an environment that fosters their child's emotional growth, maturation, and internal resilience. Although nothing replaces the calming effects of nature, parents can do their best to keep these key ingredients alive in the home. I've written about these approaches in my first two books, *The Parallel Process* and *Brave Parenting*.

BRAVE TEACHING

As a parent coach and parenting author, I see more and more parenting books each year about helicopter parents, over-involved parents, over-parenting, and the like. Furthermore, these books aren't only about troubled children who have fallen behind; they concern parents of children who go to selective colleges: Middlebury (*Parenting in a Time of Anxiety*) and Stanford (*How to Raise an Adult*). As enmeshed, over-involved parenting and student problems grow, very little discussion is taking place on how these impact schools and teachers.

Colleges to some degree have adapted to the parents of millennials by creating special programs for parents on how to establish boundaries with their young adult children (whom many parents are texting every day). But what about elementary, middle, and high schools? Teachers in these settings are dealing with over-eager and over-anxious parents. What is the best way for elementary-, middle-, and high-school teachers to enable their students' maturation and work with their demanding, hovering parents?

Schools are now on the front lines of the helicopter epidemic, because parents mostly don't realize they are hovering and over-steering until, well, many years of hovering and steering. Parents think, just like Sarah did, that they are advocating for and protecting their kids. The evidence of how these strategies backfire becomes glaringly apparent in junior high or high school. Yet the results of enmeshed parenting are observable in much younger children and tend to be played out in elementary schools, youth sports, youth dance, and other extracurricular activities.

Even pre-school and kindergarten teachers see this, such as when parents ask why their child only got a check: "What needs to be done to get the check-plus?" Rather than viewing school as a place of learning and skill-development, parents want high achievement and success right away. Teachers see parents "paving the way" for their child long before the parents realize this could be problematic behavior. Parents then want to micro-manage their child's teacher so the teacher can do the same for their child's success.

Parents have yet to learn the hard truth that "paving the way" only fosters dependency, parent–child power struggles, delayed maturation, and in some cases defiance, anxiety, depression, or substance abuse, among other mental health conditions. These outcomes are, of course, exactly the opposite of what parents want. For kids already with sensitivities such as ADD, anxiety, learning issues, anger problems, or who are on the spectrum, "paving the way" further prevents them from developing internal resources and self-regulation skills because they are being even more externally managed by parents and other adults. Teachers have the unique ability to intervene earlier to foster independent skill-development in school, educate parents on helicoptering and its negative outcomes, and create a culture of emotional growth, accountability, and resilience.

Teachers are fortunate to be able to see children horizontally (at a particular moment), whereas parents see their children longitudinally (over time). As a result, teachers can pick up in a few minutes what parent–child patterns may be at play and not serving the child (or parent!). Examples might include: parents organizing their child's backpack, correcting their child's homework before turning it in, stopping by the school to drop off a forgotten lunch or pair of soccer cleats, or even taking over a child's science project (it happens!). These activities certainly reflect an engaged parent; however, they may disable the child from organizing his own backpack; hide what the child *didn't* know in her homework; stop the child from learning to remember what he needs to bring to school each morning; or remove the child's responsibility for her own learning.

In 2016, I spoke at an elementary/middle school (pre-K–8) in Delaware and was heartened to see the school displaying the motto "This is a no rescue school" as you entered. Such an idea runs counter to many public messages, where "good" parenting entails performing an action. In this case, the school's model of parenting or teaching promotes a non-action. This school embraced students' internal skill-development. It wasn't trying to "pave the way," but instead to let kids stumble over and around the rocks and boulders on their path. This is the very philosophy endorsed by wilderness programs, where struggle is valued and not dismissed.

Can teachers be frontline change agents in emotional growth, maturation, and internal skill-development *without* feeling it's yet one more thing to check off on their never-ending list of subjects to cover each year? I believe the answer is *Yes* and *No*. Certainly, this book brings more awareness to yet *another* issue for teachers to deal with. But the truth is that teachers are *already* dealing with this problem: every day with kids, and every night with parents (who might be emailing their teachers).

What if teachers had more tools in their belt to address internal skill-development, emotional resiliency, and maturation? What if schools valued these inner skills and instead of steering kids toward success, allowed safe struggle? What if kids learned to solve problems in life (friends, homework, and emotional regulation) and not just in math class? What if kids were taught accountability very young, so they could know that ownership of their feelings and behaviors was empowering, because they were in charge of themselves? What if kids learned to self-regulate through mindfulness, breathing techniques, and assertive communication? These skills are outlined in this book.

Today, there is an epidemic of young adults at home without the necessary maturation to live independently. Parents frequently report to me, "I got my child through high school, but he or she struggled hard in college." Yet, these parents make the situation worse by standing over their children and their school assignments and managing everything else: household chores, laundry, cooking, organizing, carpooling, and so on. Kids are expected to excel in a few narrow areas (academics, sports, music) while everything else is taken care of.

Indeed, many kids today go to university only to return home because they don't have the executive functioning and/or emotional self-regulation to deal with college. Or if a child stays in college, many parents are *still* entrenched in their lives: texting daily, steering decision-making, solving problems, managing finances, rescuing their children from a bind, attending course-registration days—even accompanying them on job interviews. Kids aren't living independently in or out of college. The electronic tethers keep children front and center in their parents' lives.

The cost of all this is a lack of differentiation between a child's and a parent's life. The cost is childhood extending to age twenty-five or thirty. The cost is the kid's mental and emotional health as he or she lacks the skills needed to navigate independently, which in turn creates more anxiety, depression, and apathy. If this isn't addressed in schools, parents will continue to want to manage teachers and their child's learning in a way that fosters more dependency rather than independent skill-development.

———

I WORKED WITH pre-adolescents, adolescents, and young adults in wilderness programs for more than a decade. I saw withdrawn kids engage and defiant kids learn to follow rules. Children talked about their feelings rather than acted them out. Socially anxious young people formed genuine friendships, and those who were highly dependent on their parents grew more capable and self-reliant. Anxious kids who hid emotionally came forward and revealed who they were. I saw how all emotions had to be valued, all behaviors needed to be accounted for, and how safe struggle was necessary for kids to mature. "Problem kids" became emotional leaders.

We wilderness instructors and therapists felt a bit like magicians, as kids transformed in front of our eyes. It was grueling work when kids were at their worst: defiant, shut down, and refusing to engage; or quick to anger or self-pity. Over time, however, it became clear to us that essential wilderness ingredients, when combined, produced emotional maturation. Because most kids had some delay in their emotional development, the experience of the wilderness helped them grow up. This book brings that special magic to teachers!

Schools can interrupt this parenting epidemic with "no-rescue" schools. Teachers can be trained to build skills in their students to help them be self-reliant, capable, and accountable for themselves. What an incredible shift for kids to learn to master their internal environment, so they can have energy available for learning content and expanding their intellect! How do teachers do this? Through fostering learning containers where they employ the magic ingredients. In the remainder of this book, I teach the concepts and provide real examples of how simple shifts dramatically improve the classroom culture and the learning environment, not to mention collaboration with parents and the larger school community.

chapter 2

THE CLASSROOM CONTAINER

Bringing Together the Four Essential Ingredients

.

REALIZING I WAS ten minutes late after getting caught in Denver's morning rush, I hurried across the parking lot into Sarah Love's school. I assumed that by observing all day, I'd be interrupting her teaching already, and I thought I might have missed an opportunity to talk before school started. I was wrong. Sarah greeted me without any rush, and after we met her fourth-grade students in the front of the school, the students (all twenty-two of them) proceeded to follow their Friday morning routine, without *any* prompting from Sarah.

Astonished, I watched the students put their belongings away in their cubbies, quietly walk into the classroom, and begin their three Friday-morning tasks: journaling about something that happened that week, taking a spelling quiz (via iPad and headset as different students are at different levels), and writing an email to their parents about their week at school. Sarah explained these assignments to me and remarked, "The parents really love the Friday email, because the students are the reporters rather than the teachers. Plus, the email gives the family something to discuss over the weekend. It opens lines of communication between the student and the parent regarding school and schoolwork."

As Sarah was talking to me, she placed a button on the board and turned a light on. Soon a student came up to ask a question: "Can we write about Halloween in our essay?" Sarah pointed at the light. I then read what it said: MS. LOVE IS BUSY. ASK A FRIEND. This student swiftly turned around and asked the question of a neighbor at her table. I thought this button was brilliant on many levels. As parents, teachers, and caregivers today, we think we need always to be available to our kids and to answer *all* their questions, frequently interrupting what we're doing to give attention to kids. Yet, in doing this we're disrupting children's ability to be resourceful and solve problems. Sarah explained: "Yes, I want my classroom to be collaborative problem-solvers. I don't think the teacher always has the answer. When I put this light on, I want them to work together and come up with their own answers. It helps to develop critical thinking."

I continued to be amazed at how self-sufficient and self-directed this diverse group of nine-year-olds was and how available Sarah was to talk with me about her teaching and how she had incorporated *Brave Parenting* into her class and the school at large. As the students completed their three tasks, they left their tables and sat quietly in a circle on the rug. I then had an opportunity to talk with them about why I was there.

"Are you the author?" one asked.

"Yes, and thanks for having me visit your classroom today. How are things going with Ms. Love this year?"

"Good." They all nodded positively and attentively.

"You may not be aware," I continued, "as you did not have her last year, but Ms. Love is bringing the concepts of my books into the classroom with all of you. In my background, I have worked with kids who were struggling with their emotions and their behaviors. How many of you at times feel sad, mad, or worried?" I raised my hand and most of the class did the same. "Well, all of your feelings are normal and OK. It is part of being human. The problem is more your behavior. Do any of you get mad at home and slam the door to your room?"

Most started to laugh and nodded that they did.

"Is it a good choice to slam your door?"

There was a resounding *No!* through the group.

"Exactly. That is what Ms. Love is teaching: to give you the safety and space to feel, but asking you to take ownership of your behaviors. How do you feel about yourself when you slam a door?"

One girl's arm shot up. "Not good," she said when I called on her.

"Right," I responded. "It doesn't feel good when we make a choice to act out. It might feel good for one minute, but usually five minutes later it doesn't feel as good. The most important thing is to let yourself feel what you feel, until it passes."

After a few more questions from the group, the students lined up for a music class and were led out of the room. With very few words, Sarah was holding her presence in the classroom, and it was clear she'd created an independent classroom and school in session after only three months. The students were all self-directed and seemed safe and secure in their classroom and engaged in their learning. Sarah had effectively created a learning container that held the four essential ingredients. This is the essence of Brave Teaching.

THE LEARNING CONTAINER

The learning container is the environment where the four essential ingredients for internal skill-development are implemented. Although teaching specific skills is important, and we'll get into them in Part 2, the learning container is more about creating an everyday culture of emotional accountability, behavioral ownership, and problem-solving for *all* learning.

The combination of these ingredients promotes the emotional maturity and resiliency that were evident in the wilderness setting. In fact, any environment where these four ingredients are present can be a container for maturation, whether it's a wilderness program, a home, a sports team, a classroom, a school, and so on. Internal skills are fostered and developed when these four ingredients are present.

THE FOUR ESSENTIAL INGREDIENTS

1) Emotional Attunement
2) Behavioral Boundaries and Accountability
3) Valuing Struggle
4) Safety

All these ingredients will be elaborated in their own chapters, but an overview follows here:

1) *Emotional Attunement*

I learned in wilderness therapy that underneath *all* behavior or *any* acting out is an emotion. Most teachers deal with children's behavior in the classroom setting every day. Emotional attunement is the process of recognizing students' emotions or feeling states and "mirroring" them. These emotions are then validated and valued as important information. Mirroring involves seeing and reflecting the child's emotion or digging underneath the child's behavior for the child's feeling, and then holding that feeling as precious and valuable. If we do this, kids are much more likely to share and *much* less likely to act out their feelings through behaviors (to get attention). The adult holds up a metaphorical mirror to reflect the student's emotions. This conveys the message, "I see you."

For example, a teacher might say: "Your tone sounds upset. Can you tell me what you're feeling?" (*mirroring*); "That sounds like it's frustrating" (*validating*); "I can see that you're feeling sad. Your feelings are important. I'm here if you'd like to share" (*attuned and validating*); "I notice that you're fidgeting your hands. Are you feeling nervous? That's a really normal response to taking a test" (*attuning and normalizing*).

Emotional attunement acknowledges and creates space for feelings. In our society, especially for teachers, we're afraid to acknowledge feelings, as we fear the acknowledgment will make those feelings greater by drawing attention to them. However, just the opposite happens (Try it!). When kids feel heard and acknowledged, they move on much more quickly. Likewise, when emotions are overlooked, many kids escalate them to be heard. Teachers might also think that acknowledging a feeling means the child is "right." Emotional attunement, however, recognizes only the feeling, which is neither right nor wrong. *Behaviors* are what can be identified as good/bad or right/wrong. This distinction is the most critical component of the skill-building I learned in wilderness therapy.

Emotions simply give us important information. They are not something to fix or change, but to identify, validate, and allow. When we validate a child's feeling we empathize with them. The fundamental ethos to wilderness therapy is that when kids talk about feelings, they are much less likely to act them out. In schools, we tend to focus on the behavior; what would happen if we nurtured and valued the emotion instead?

For example, Mrs. S. might say to a student (we'll call him Tommy): "Hitting Jonny at recess is not an OK choice of behavior." (*Choice* is an important word to use, because many kids feel like things "just happen.") "But I imagine that you were feeling a big emotion. Can you tell me what it was?"

"Mad," Tommy whispers.

"OK," responds Mrs. S. "'Mad' is an important feeling and one that definitely needs attention and care. I wonder what you can do the next time you feel mad?" (Mrs. S. is letting the child problem-solve.)

"I guess talk to a teacher about my feeling?"

"Yes, that would be a great strategy. I get mad a lot, too, and I find that telling someone safe helps me calm down."

Tommy nods.

"What would you like to do to repair things with Jonny? You know any physical interaction is against our school rules."

"I guess apologize. But what about what he did to me?"

"Well, that is for him to own. All you are responsible for is for taking care of your emotions and owning your behaviors."

"OK." Tommy nods and runs off back to recess.

The identification and validation of feelings bring awareness and relief. When kids can identify their feelings, teachers can listen and give healthy coping options, such as going to a "sit spot" to take deep breaths, doing a feelings check with a teacher, creating art, or taking a walk around the field or through a building. These coping skills teach kids to own their feelings and to self-regulate. When kids do this instead of blaming others, they learn a fundamental lesson about inner freedom. I've seen this over and over again in the wilderness: kids stop blaming their parents, take responsibility for their own behavior, and fully accept how their parents chose to raise them. The children then direct their energy toward their lives and learning instead of fighting with their parents. Furthermore, when students are heard and validated they're much more likely to hold themselves accountable for their behavior.

I was able to observe Sarah's attentive listening and how she held the space for kids' emotions rather than trying to fix them. This is a substantial adjustment, as most adults want to solve children's problems. However, I could see how secure the kids felt and how open they were with her. They knew Ms. Love wouldn't tell them what to do; instead, she'd ask them to problem-solve. Kids don't actually want solutions from adults. However, they *do* want to be heard and validated. (I didn't observe any students using emotional escalation to get attention or their way, because clearly such approaches didn't work on Ms. Love. Interestingly, I *did* observe kids doing this in the sixth-grade classroom, which I describe later.)

2) *Behavioral Boundaries and Accountability*
Behavioral boundaries provide the structure of the learning container. Remember: all feelings are OK, validated, and accepted, but not all behaviors are acceptable. So, it's critical for students to know what those behaviors are, if they cross a line, and how they'll be held accountable.

For example, whereas it's acceptable for a child to *feel* frustrated, angry, and upset, it's not OK for him or her to use inappropriate language in the classroom, to hurt other kids, or to lie or cheat.

Boundaries also help create order and predictability, which increase safety and reduce anxiety for students. The students know that if a child is disruptive, he or she will be held to an accountability measure.

An accountability measure or consequence is *very* different from a punishment. The former holds someone responsible and separates the person from the behavior. Whereas a punishment implies the *person* is bad, an accountability measure implies that the *choice* is bad, unsafe, or inappropriate. By valuing a child for his or her feeling and holding him or her accountable for a choice, you are removing the shame from the situation, unlike with punishment, which can provoke feelings of shame. This distinction is critical. It's my belief that society's fear of punishment that provokes shame has led to the reduction and removal of disciplinary and accountability measures in schools and homes.

The wilderness taught me that accountability can be rendered in a way that is effective at promoting maturation and clearing a child's conscience. For example, when a teen steals and then does community service as a consequence, the slate can be cleaned. By contrast, in my experience of working with teens, when parents don't hold the child accountable for lying because they don't want him or her to feel bad, most kids still harbor negative feelings about themselves and their choices because they didn't have to make any reparation. Without accountability, teens remain stuck with guilt, regret, and self-loathing. Remember: we can't fix kids' feelings, but we *can* help them make their own internal amends.

Sarah's school had a natural accountability structure already in place in the classroom. Kids had "money" in their accounts on the first day of school that could be withdrawn or deposited based on healthy or unhealthy choices. (This system was also designed to teach banking, so it had a dual focus.) Kids could earn parties or toys through the "money." Sarah believes that the system's structure held behavioral boundaries in place and taught accountability in a non-shaming and empowering way.

Since Sarah has employed the concepts from *Brave Parenting*, she's noticed behavioral problems drop away. This result is largely due to her incorporating emotional attunement. Maintaining appropriate boundaries is much more effective when kids' emotions are validated first. Many teachers yell or sigh when they're frustrated with kids. But reacting with emotions is neither effective parenting nor teaching, since it only lets kids know they have power over adults. When structure and accountability are in place, teachers need not fear being rattled by kids, because they know they can always hold a child accountable. (Sometimes, teachers still need to do their own self-regulation. Stepping away to take a few deep breaths can be essential.) Then come the ownership of behavior and solving problems that Sarah has integrated into all her teaching.

One pleasant side-effect of Sarah's incorporation of *Brave Parenting* techniques is that parents love what's occurring in the classroom. She's reported to me that she hasn't received a single email from parents since the second week of school. (We discuss teacher interactions with parents later.)

As a parent coach, I worked with a tenth-grader (whom I'll call Jeff). Jeff attended a high school in California and felt strongly that homework was optional. Although he performed adequately in school, he never completed or handed in any homework. In high schools, the "natural consequence" of kids not completing their assignments during the year would be summer school. Jeff had already completed summer school the previous year and was heading in that direction again. Jeff's mother wanted to give her son a more immediate consequence for his inaction.

After working with Jeff's mother and his teacher, I devised a plan whereby Jeff's teacher emailed his mother each Friday to let her know if Jeff had any outstanding homework. If he did, Jeff's parents held him accountable by removing his weekend social privileges. Although Jeff didn't like this and wanted to rebel more, he adjusted. Because the consequence was more immediate, he took notice and began creating time for homework. This behavioral boundary (holding him accountable for homework) dramatically improved Jeff's school engagement, grades, and overall self-esteem.

3) *Valuing Struggle*

Valuing struggle is exactly what it means: recognizing that something may be difficult and require effort to overcome, but that both are critical to the learning process. The current parenting paradigm is to remove or mitigate difficulty in our children's lives—including by hovering over schools. Although such behavior stems from care and concern, what is visible across the spectrum is that children today lack the skills to cope adequately with discomfort, disappointments, challenges, and complications. Instead, they look to adults to fix and solve their problems, or act helpless or blame others for their struggles.

Struggle is *essential* to learning, so we shouldn't consider kids' frustrations socially, academically, or behaviorally negatively. This is hard. I watched my daughter experience horrible, subtle bullying and social exclusion in the fifth and sixth grades, and I found it almost impossible to find value in her troubles. However, she is one-hundred percent more mature, compassionate, and resilient because of them. She's learned skills and developed a self-awareness I could never have taught her, since she had to undergo that period. The fact that I reframed what she had to go through positively—by letting her understand that struggle was normal, validating her feelings, and making sure she knew that the difficulties held important lessons for her—certainly helped.

Struggle not only helps kids problem-solve but also develop other "internal skills"—such as healthy coping, assertive communication, delayed gratification, emotional self-regulation, and conflict resolution. Without struggle, there'd be no need to develop these skills, which are needed in our adult lives. Why would we not want to teach them to kids? Unconsciously, we want to create a bubble of happiness, success, and fun for kids today (I am certainly guilty of this desire), but the bubble doesn't prepare them at all for adulthood.

Certainly, some kids may require extra services (like reading support or a math tutor) to achieve, but if we reframe struggle as an opportunity to build skills, we shift the energy and reactivity that kids and adults may feel. After all, students can't learn to problem-solve unless they're experiencing problems that need a solution.

One student in Sarah's class I'll call Henry seemed to fall apart in the last few periods of the day. He habitually somaticized his emotions by complaining of headaches, stomach-aches, and sore throats. He frequently went to the nurse or even home early. To bring in some accountability, Sarah had Henry sign out of the classroom and sign in every time he went to the nurse. After a few weeks, Sarah sat down with Henry and looked at the sign-in sheet and asked if he was aware of how much he was going to the nurse. Henry was not, so the pair of them discussed other options for him to take care of himself. How could he problem-solve what he felt?

I was able to observe one of these afternoon interactions. Henry looked tired and told Ms. Love he wasn't feeling well.

"OK. What are you feeling?" Sarah asked empathically.

"My throat hurts."

"Do you have any emotions there also?"

"I feel tired and a little anxious."

"OK. Thanks for telling me how you feel. How do you want to solve this?"

"Well, I don't think I need to go home," said Henry. "And I don't think I need to go to the nurse, so I think I will get a drink of water. Can I go to my cubby to get my water bottle?"

"Of course," Sarah responded. "It sounds like a choice that might help."

My jaw almost hit the floor. Again, although the solution to the problem seemed minor, I saw Henry's decision as an enormous act of self-care. Many *adults* don't problem-solve this well! As parents, we tell kids to drink water all the time, to no avail. Here was a clear example of a teacher tuning into an emotion, allowing the student to feel, and then asking him to figure out a solution. Henry did this without any suggestions from an adult. Because of his ownership of the problem and solution, Henry was empowered and much less likely to act out his feelings by going home early or visiting the nurse and creating further difficulties related to avoidance and missing school. Sarah helped Henry accept discomfort and struggle and learn to take care of himself by the simple yet necessary act of drinking water.

4) *Safety*

General safety is a no-brainer for teachers. Nonetheless, it's essential, since none of the other ingredients will work if the environment is not safe. Safety refers not only to physical security, but emotional welfare as well. For physical and emotional safety, there must be rules, with adults in charge, leading and setting the tone. An emotionally safe environment requires teachers to be in their teaching authority.

We might characterize safe authority as command: a pilot in charge of a plane (not the passengers), a parent in charge of the household (not the children), and a teacher in charge of a classroom (not the students). When the figure in command doesn't establish safe authority, non-authority figures set the tone. Although this situation may be exciting, it diminishes a sense of security. For example, if a pilot makes an executive decision to fly through turbulence instead of rerouting the plane, he or she can calm passengers by informing them of the decision so the latter feel safe. If the pilot seems unsure or non-communicative in his or her authority, passengers will likely react with anxiety or stress. Likewise, if a teacher sets rules and maintains order in a classroom, he or she will create more safety and predictability. If kids are more in control of a classroom, it might feel more chaotic and less safe.

There is a correlation between order, predictability, and safety, and, likewise, disorder, unpredictability, insecurity, and anxiety. Structure and daily routines are good for children because they create security and make schools feel safe.

Inconsistent boundaries and/or a lack of parental authority have contributed to the rise in children's anxiety. Kids today possess more choices in their lives, choices that many find beyond their mental and emotional development to make. A number of parents have confessed to me that their child acts like the CEO of the home, and everything is a negotiation. This "transfer of power," whereby the child has a lot of say in what happens, is frequently paired with entitlement, and both actually create more anxiety for kids. Kids lack the prefrontal cortex development for the level of choice in their lives, and aren't emotionally mature enough to hold equal power with adults, let alone more.

Paradoxically, when kids express that anxiety, parents offer them *even more* choices: "You don't have to go to soccer if you don't feel like it"; "OK, I'll make another dinner"; "If you have a lot of homework, I can do your chore for you." Parents don't back away from boundaries because they are pushovers but because they're worried about their child's stress and mental health. Parents first and foremost want contented kids in a close relationship with them. We think giving kids power and choice will make them happy.

So, a negative cycle begins: choice increases anxiety, anxiety increases more choice. Gray areas don't make kids happy; they create wiggle-room and stress and reduce accountability. I've seen depressed, anxious, and unhappy kids in the wilderness discover an internal happiness that comes from applying themselves in life: completing a tough hike, starting their first fire, sharing something with their peers, and preparing a meal for the group. Real happiness comes from engagement and completion, not from having a way out. Real happiness can only emerge from safe, consistent, and secure boundaries.

When teachers give up power or authority in the classroom, they're more likely to respond to students with irritation—a consequence of feeling powerless to change the situation. They may even blame the student for frustrating them. In actuality, the students are responding to the lack of structure, accountability, and teacher authority. Students tend to "test" limits when there's a gray area. This then looks like acting out, which, in turn, spurs annoyance and even a power struggle.

It was clear in Sarah's classroom that the structure and norms had established teacher authority and, therefore, emotional safety.

The schedule and routine had created a predictability that allowed the kids to feel productive and engaged. This in turn had developed esteem. Sarah's students trusted her enough to tell her their feelings. That esteem was also observable in how open the children were with me, a visitor, about their emotions. The children also knew that Sarah wouldn't do for them what they could do for themselves. That meant she respected them. Their happiness was apparent as they took pride in their independence to problem-solve on their own.

When adults are in charge and set the tone, an emotionally safe classroom is created. When anything "unsafe" arises—such as bullying, defiance, or even struggling in learning—the issue is identified and responded to intentionally by safe adults.

MIXING THE ESSENTIAL INGREDIENTS

Now that we have the Four Ingredients—emotional attunement, behavioral boundaries and accountability, valuing struggle, and safety—we need to mix them and stir. Their combination promotes internal skill-development, maturation, accountability, and emotional resilience.

It should be noted that unless all four ingredients are present, we don't have a learning container. If emotional attunement is missing, it's impossible to have safe struggle and emotional safety, and behavioral boundaries are much less effective. If behavioral boundaries are absent, no safe norms are set and there's no student accountability, which would create chaos and reduce safety. If safe struggle isn't there, students will either act helpless or dependent, or experience unsafe struggle. Lastly, without teacher authority creating safety, all the other ingredients will be undermined. It's the critical mix of these four ingredients that creates the perfect environment to promote skill-development and emotional maturation. Every learning container needs to have these four ingredients, even though some classrooms might have larger amounts of some ingredients than the others. This is what teachers can assess.

When the ingredients are in balance, a flow environment is created that fosters all learning. Although it may sound overwhelming to create the learning container, only relatively minor shifts about building new norms in the classroom routine that target internal skill-development in the students are required.

Schools can teach these invaluable skills today, rather than leaving them to parents. Parents may unknowingly interrupt the development of these skills through their hovering: by fixing problems, rescuing emotions, mitigating struggle, removing obstacles, and working hard behind the scenes to "pave the way" for success. Whatever approach parents are taking at home, teachers can bring the Four Ingredients into their classrooms and schools. Furthermore, classrooms can run like well-oiled machines, where the best is coming out of kids and thornier problems tend to fall by the wayside. In the following chapters, we dive deeper into each essential ingredient and fine-tune the strategies that teachers can bring to their classrooms.

part 1

THE FOUR ESSENTIAL INGREDIENTS

chapter 3

INGREDIENT #1—EMOTIONAL ATTUNEMENT

Working with Children's Emotions

WHILE I WAS observing other classrooms and interacting with students at Sarah Love's school, I met Penny, a studious and shy student in the sixth grade. She told me that she'd been born in India and had lived in the United States since she was two. I noticed that she was quite stylish in her matching skirt and boots. In Penny's classroom of twenty-six students, I encountered commotion, side conversations, and many kids who appeared to be in their own world. The students were supposed to be working on revising their individual essays after receiving peer comments on their Google docs. The teacher, Mrs. G., sat behind her desk and frequently shouted out, "*Focus!*"

I could *feel* the change from Sarah's classroom. Although Mrs. G. was kind and caring with the students, she lacked authority and presence, and remaining behind the desk didn't enforce either. The sixth-graders seemed to be walking all over her by doing what they wanted, without any apparent accountability.

Amidst the hubbub, a frightened Penny came up to Mrs. G.'s desk and told her she couldn't find her jean jacket that had her phone in the pocket. The class seemed chaotic at this point, and the volume of side conversations rose higher and higher. Mrs. G. told Penny to announce to the class that her jacket was missing. Penny walked to the front of the white-board. Due to her mounting distress, Penny covered her face with her hands and began to cry. She wasn't able to talk. All twenty-five other students stopped and looked up. Two of Penny's friends ran up to hug her. They held her in a dramatic display and, as she choked back tears, Penny whispered that she'd lost her jean jacket and asked if anyone had seen it. She then left the classroom to walk the halls, while her two friends hovered over her. The teacher let her go outside because she seemed so upset.

I saw that although Mrs. G. was asking Penny to solve the problem, she missed a critical opportunity to attune her emotions to Penny's distress. What then transpired was what occurs in most schools, families, workplaces, and so on: the emotional rescue. Kids learn at very young ages that if they escalate their emotions, they will get the attention of adults and will most likely be rescued from their distress. Instead of teaching ownership, accountability, and self-regulation for our feelings, we reward kids today when they gin up their emotions. Adults frequently backpedal from rules, expectations, or boundaries in an attempt to soothe a child's distress. Penny was allowed to leave the class with her friends because she was upset.

Instead of teaching emotional self-regulation regularly or consistently to children, adults tend to get mad at kids when they escalate their emotions, or they rescue them. Neither approach helps kids learn how to handle their feelings. Moreover, when kids become unable to control themselves, adults tend to be triggered and can lose control as well. The result is a conflagration that only feeds itself. Instead, adults need to be like water. We need to work on staying present, calm, and non-reactive in the face of kids' emotional upheavals.

LEARNING SELF-REGULATION

Fortunately, in my early twenties and before I became a parent, I had an opportunity to work on regulating myself and learn the profound skill of emotional attunement. (Although I was grateful to learn these skills as a young adult, ideally students could learn these skills today when they're even younger.) I was fresh out of college when I was employed in the innovative wilderness-therapy program that worked with children who had gotten into trouble. Instead of going to a youth detention center, these kids were sent to the middle of nowhere Utah to learn outdoor skills, do group therapy, and understand their emotions and behaviors. I was a very green field instructor, and one of the activities we performed daily—sometimes three times a day—was a feelings check.

I usually knew what I felt if I experienced a big emotion that interrupted my day, such as sadness about a relationship, worry about a test I had to take or a race I was to run, or frustration about a situation. But I never learned the skill of simply "tuning in" to my emotions when nothing in particular seemed to be happening. We gathered in a circle, and each person in the group (staff included) had to identify a "feeling word" that best described their current emotion. I'd learned through years of achievement to analyze my environment and others, and what they expected of me. I had almost never stopped to read my *inner* environment. I stumbled through this life-altering skill along with the angry, distraught teenagers.

I noticed I tended to want to say I was "fine," but knew this was not an emotion. I had to dig deeper. Sometimes, I felt "calm" or "relief" if we were sitting down to lunch or had just arrived at camp after a long hike. However, most frequently I was uneasy. I noticed a background feeling of anxiety, like white noise, crackling behind my thoughts. I had to be honest and model for the kids in the group. So, I frequently shared that I was "anxious," "worried," or "tense." It was liberating not to have to explain my feelings or tell some story about what was happening, but instead simply to share what was real for me. Whenever I was truthful and genuine, the kids nodded, as though authenticity had established a connection between us.

Nonetheless, I didn't let myself off the hook so easily. Because I'd been a high achiever in sports and school, I started to judge this negative emotion in me. Why was I feeling so anxious? Aside from being intimidated and in over my head working with these troubled kids, I knew anxiety was a longer-term emotion for me. Certainly, no one was judging me; in fact, the group was more accepting of me the more honest I was. I was judging myself. As we continued this exercise of feelings checks week in and week out, I realized I had to practice what we were preaching. I had to stop the self-judgment. I wanted to be more curious; in fact, I wanted to be that person who was *self-aware*.

Since then, I've been on a personal and professional journey to get to know my feelings—with curiosity, awareness, and ownership, rather than judgment or self-rejection. The minute we reject our inner landscape, we go right to blame. I could find all sorts of things to blame my anxiety on: the group of difficult kids I was working with, not liking the other staff members, wishing I was out of the field and able to eat more fresh food, and so on. Blame, I learned, is disempowering. However, through paying attention, I began to see I experienced low-lying anxiety outside the field on my days off, too. Of course, I attributed my anxiety to other things: relationships, money, my living situation, and so on. But my self-inquiry continued. This led to awareness, and then to ownership (not blame), and then to self-care. Through feelings checks, I learned to look after my inner self. I was the only one who experienced my emotion; it was not someone's fault. Although blaming someone or something else has been convenient to me at times, I realize that tuning into and caretaking my feelings are my responsibility.

Over many years of feelings checks with my inner environment, I've gained an internal power I never could have achieved through being focused outward. I began to think: *What if we taught this to younger kids, and* all *kids—not just those in trouble with the courts or in some type of therapy? Adults need it, too.*

THE RIVER OF EMOTIONS

At every moment of our waking lives, an emotional river runs through us. Whether we might describe it as tired, worried, scared, calm, relaxed, tense, anxious, happy, excited, peaceful, frustrated, angry, disappointed, afraid, sad, embarrassed, or satisfied, the river keeps flowing. Emotions are like our internal navigation system. When we stop and take its measure, our emotional river offers wonderful information to help us steer our lives. For example, anxiety could be a prompt to take some deep breaths, maybe go for a walk or exercise. Anger (after de-escalation) can be a principal indicator for making a change, setting a limit, or telling someone *No*. Sadness can relate to deeper feelings of love, fear, and loss. It's vital we recognize and feel these emotions.

Rather than listening to our emotions, however, we too often ignore them, distract ourselves from them, and/or (most commonly) judge them. Self-judgment, the inner critic, and negative self-talk are pervasive. We frequently project this inner negativity and blame something outside ourselves as being the source of this emotion, and ignore the precious innate gift of the emotional river. That current gives our inner lives richness and texture, just like the color spectrum brings our world to life. We don't place value judgments on yellow or blue, yet we frequently think happy is "good" and sad is "bad." But responding to our emotional rivers can give us information at any moment to allow us to self-regulate and have care for what we feel. In fact, "negative" emotions can help guide our lives the most, since they let us know where and how we're stuck and that some action needs to happen. If we were happy all the time, we'd be unlikely to make changes. Life would not be interesting, and would most likely be boring!

Unfortunately, emotional attunement or self-attunement isn't taught in our society. In fact, our culture encourages us to impede the flow. I learned through my own personal work that the reason I was carrying around low-grade anxiety was that I had dammed much of my inner life, causing emotional pressure to build up. My parents, though well-meaning, seemed to live as though emotions didn't exist, so my feelings could never be attuned to, acknowledged, and validated. As a result, I learned to dam, or shut off, my own river—although not completely.

We dam (stop or control) an emotion by finding an escape through food, alcohol, drugs, technology, or materialism. Or we do it by trying to control ourselves and others, gossiping, blaming, embracing victim-hood, and so on. These emotional disconnections are everywhere.

Adults who dam their emotions, which is most of us, frequently then want to do the same with their children's feelings. Kids' upsets, tantrums, sadness, and worry get to us; they trigger the emotions we're working hard to keep at bay. Whether we're a parent, teacher, or both, we tend to want to fix and change children's intense emotions. We think we're helping, but in fact we're trying to control them. For all of our conscious practices raising and teaching kids, very little intention is placed on children's emotions. We tend to skip over them in search of "happy." When the emotion is anything other than happiness, we respond in a knee-jerk manner or as if on auto-pilot—the opposite of intentional. As a result, when kids get worked up, we tend to get triggered also, either internally (invisibly) and/or externally (visibly).

LETTING KIDS FEEL AND TEACHING OWNERSHIP

When we let children feel, we remove the dams and allow kids to under-stand their emotions are safe, normal, and significant. As I indicated in the Introduction, anxiety is not the problem; anxiety *and refusing to go to school* is. If a child is sad, all we need to do is listen, validate, and allow the emotion to pass: no problem. If that sadness is accompanied by a meltdown and disrespect to Mom: problem. The problem is not the emotion, but the *behavior*. Emotions can certainly be exaggerated, as in a tantrum, but I would consider that behavior. Feeling upset about not getting candy at the store is an ordinary, human emotion. Kicking, screaming, and abuse aren't. Separating feeling from behavior is critical when it comes to ownership and awareness.

When we let kids feel, we allow their emotional currents to flow. Instead of ignoring their emotions, or damming, fixing, or judging them, we can encourage our children to feel. A mother of three recently told me: "I believe that in my generation of parenting we have been taught to deal with children's feelings by distracting them, and now they're all addicted to screens. Wow! I realized I never just let my kids just feel sad or worried or bored. No wonder they don't know how to be with their emotions."

When we remove the dam and let kids feel, the response can be, "That sounds like an important emotion to feel!" Not many adults say this, but it's a huge shift. When kids learn to allow the flow, since all emotions are transient, they not only discover self-regulation but also emotional resiliency.

The aim of emotional attunement is for teachers to be aware not only of their own inner landscape but also the emotions of their students. Once you're attuned to a student, you can validate his or her emotion, and allow the child to feel. "Mirroring," which we touched on earlier, is a technique that reflects only what would be visible in a mirror or heard by three people. In other words, the technique involves observation and not inference. I've learned that teachers can "mirror" anything. Therefore, unless a child is completely content and rational, mirroring is a great tool to bring awareness to a child's emotions or behaviors and ask kids to be accountable.

If a child (for instance, Tommy) stomps his feet through the classroom, a teacher can mirror the gesture. "Tommy, I can hear you stomping your feet. Are you feeling upset?"

"No," he answers, with a scowl on his face.

"OK. Well, that behavior is disruptive in the classroom. If you are feeling upset about something, I am happy to check in with you."

Tommy doesn't share, but he *does* stop stomping his feet.

Though this might seem insignificant, a lot has occurred here. This teacher sees, attunes, acknowledges feelings, and creates space for Tommy to feel. Tommy chooses not to share, but I'm guessing he feels seen, and *could* be heard if he chose to speak. What is most significant is that Tommy also chooses to stop stomping his feet, which is self-regulation. It's clear to me after years of adolescent therapy and parent coaching that kids do not want to "win" or "be right." They want to been seen and heard. Mirroring is very effective at showing kids what they're doing and this frequently leads to a self-adjustment.

STEPS TO MIRRORING

1) *Reflect what is observable*: It's vital *not* to say things like, "I know you're upset at Jen." That is an inference. Or, "I understand how you feel," as kids will quickly tell you that you don't. Instead, you can mirror: "I heard you raise your voice with Jen. What are you feeling?"

2) *Be specific*: "Your tone sounds very upset. Do you want to check in?" "I noticed when I asked about your homework, you looked at the ground. Is everything OK? I'm happy to go over it with you"; "I saw that you didn't present your book today. I know public speaking can be very intimidating. How are you feeling about it?"

3) *Validate/Normalize*: "It's totally normal to feel anxiety before a test. It means your body is preparing for it"; "It's sad when your friend is home sick with the flu"; "I imagine it's frustrating when you got a problem wrong that you thought you got right." Knee-jerk reactions tend to invalidate emotions: "Don't worry!" "Cheer up!" "Don't be

mad!" This response is part of the damming process. It backfires when we ask kids not to feel what they feel.

4) *Encourage ownership and problem-solving:* "I imagine it's really painful when a friend excludes you from a group. How would you like to address it?" "I hear that it's upsetting that the field trip was cancelled. I also felt upset. But now that we are back at school, it's your choice to accept the change or to continue to feel upset"; "That must be frustrating to misplace your homework. I'll let you be responsible for coming up with a strategy to keep your homework organized. I'm also here for support or ideas, too." When we empower kids to problem-solve, they are much more likely to be active solvers, rather than passive when other adults tell them how to do it.

SELF-REGULATION SKILLS

When teachers perform all these steps and a student is *still* not able to "move through" an emotion and seems stuck, it's important to teach kids some simple self-regulation skills.

Breathing: There are all sorts of breathing techniques to teach kids. Here are three for different ages/grades:

1) *K–4:* Children inhale normally while they cup their hands a few inches from their mouths. They exhale with pursed lips, as if they were blowing air into a bowl, trying to fill it with air. The long, slow exhalation triggers relaxation and letting go, and also gives the child something to focus on in the present moment, which is a mindfulness technique. Many kids who are stuck with emotions are caught in a story in their heads. Conducting a mindfulness practice brings kids out of their heads and into their bodies.

2) *3–8*: Instruct kids to breathe in through their nose and out through their mouths. Repeat this cycle five to ten times. This action also encourages the exhalation of and mindful attention to the breath. It fosters relaxation and letting go.

3) *6–Adult*: These slightly more sophisticated techniques are intended to regulate or stabilize the breath. When a child has anxiety and a racing mind, a regulating breath (such as inhaling for four counts, holding for four, and exhaling for four) can help. A relaxation/stabilizing breath entails inhaling for four, holding for seven, and exhaling for eight counts. All these are aimed at bringing awareness to the present moment, not to anxious thoughts that reside in the past or future.

Accepting what we feel

After we've taken some deep breaths, owning and accepting what we feel is a critical step in processing emotions. If we're still rejecting our feeling or blaming our emotions on someone or something, we'll remain stuck. For example, Jenna, a seventh-grader, feels really sad because she got 63 percent on her math exam. Her sadness relates to being upset about careless mistakes, but she's also frustrated the exam contained material she didn't expect. Initially, Jenna wants to blame the teacher. But through ownership, she says, "My sadness stems from feeling that I wish I did better. I accept my feeling."

Take action if there is action to take, or accept the situation if nothing can be done

Making a change if one can be made can be empowering and a way to utilize problem-solving skills. So is accepting what cannot be changed. Jenna accepted there was nothing she could do to change her grade, but she decided to take action by really understanding her mistakes, learning the material she got wrong, and realizing that this was an opportunity to learn about exam-taking for high school and college.

BRINGING EMOTIONAL ATTUNEMENT TO PENNY: A NEW ENDING

When Penny approaches Mrs. G.'s desk, clearly distressed and worried, Mrs. G. takes an opportunity to stop and attune to Penny's emotions.

"Mrs. G., I can't find my jacket anywhere," Penny says, with a panicked, shaky voice.

Mrs. G. wants to ask her to look around her area, but upon seeing Penny's emotions she pauses and mirrors what she sees: "Penny, that must be upsetting. I hate it when I lose my belongings. What are you feeling?"

"I'm really worried. My parents will be so upset if I lose my jacket and phone. They are brand new."

"Yes, I can understand that fear," Mrs. G. replies. Mrs. G. is learning to validate a child's feelings, when in the past she would have inadvertently undermined them by telling the child not to worry. But Mrs. G. has found in her training through Brave Teaching that it actually feels a lot better to feel heard and validated. When Mrs. G. listens and validates Penny, she notices that her student is slowing down and beginning to become more regulated. "Why don't you take a few breaths in through your nose and out through your mouth," Mrs. G. continues. "Try it five times." As Penny does this, everything seems to slow down more. As her emotions die down, her more rational, clear mind emerges.

"Now, would you like to problem-solve this, Penny?" Mrs. G. inquires.

"I don't know. I think I will make an announcement and ask everyone to look around their area."

"Sounds good. Let me know if there is any way I can help."

"Thanks, Mrs. G.," Penny says, as more color returns to her face.

Penny goes to the front of the class and after owning her feelings, becoming regulated, and then problem-solving, she makes an announcement about her jacket. She stands in her power and vulnerability and asks for help. The students are eager to help Penny and after some looking around, one student finds the jacket (with the phone in the pocket) by the reading corner. Penny is relieved and returns to her work.

Small incidents like these happen every day in classrooms and provide opportunities for skill-development. Taking an opportunity to mirror and attune to students and teach ownership, self-regulation, and problem-solving is providing children with a lifelong skill. Many kids today are intellectually bright but riddled with anxiety, worries, disorganization, impulsivity, and other struggles that interfere with their ability to learn and engage in school. When kids learn self-regulation, their rational minds are freed and available for learning. When students master internal resiliency, they gain confidence and esteem, which is ultimately what teachers and parents want for the young people in their charge.

chapter 4

INGREDIENT #2—BEHAVIORAL BOUNDARIES

Working with Children's Behaviors

(This chapter will discuss both normal behavior disruptions as well as children with identified behavioral struggles.)

EVERY YEAR, TEACHERS stand in front of a new class, with its different behavioral challenges. Some periods may seem relatively seamless; others may be disruptive. Yet, whatever behavioral challenges teachers face, bringing the four essential ingredients into the classroom helps kids recover quicker from upsets, allows them to be responsible for themselves and their work, and empowers teachers to make the container of the classroom a space of learning.

Gabe had received many services and had been on an individualized education plan (IEP) for mental health since preschool. He was in a self-contained behavioral-disorder (BD) classroom and had a history of meltdowns and violent conduct. Yet Gabe strived to be in a classroom setting and hated to be pulled away from his peers. So, by the time he reached fifth grade, Gabe was considered to have acquired the skills to be mainstreamed. One of Gabe's biggest struggles was the ownership of his choices. He constantly blamed others when he made an inappropriate or unsafe choice that had consequences. He would perseverate sometimes for hours because he couldn't move past the fact that he'd made a wrong choice.

Gabe was placed with Mr. Tom, a teacher with an extremely structured classroom. In the first six weeks of school, Mr. Tom provided in-depth support on ownership and problem-solving skills. Yet one day at the beginning of the year, Gabe was asked to step outside the classroom after he disrupted the lesson. Gabe then became more agitated because his teacher's assistant (TA) asked him some questions in the hall, and Gabe knew his teacher expected him to walk quietly. Gabe was angry and rigid in his thinking, so was unable to adjust to the two expectations from his teacher and his TA. As a result, Gabe refused to answer. This resulted in him losing "points," and a complete meltdown followed. Gabe sat in the hall for a good hour, emotionally venting and making it clear how victimized he was. Gabe was not able to take ownership of his choices or his emotions and thus couldn't handle the consequence.

It took Gabe almost two hours to return to being rational. During that time, Gabe's TA ignored his emotions, as he didn't want to feed into them. However, he was missing the elephant in the room. Instead, Gabe's TA did a lot of fixing: cajoling and attempting to cheer Gabe up, which didn't help Gabe regulate his emotions. Gabe's feelings were overlooked, only because his TA was not trained to work with them. Gabe eventually tired and returned to class. This is a classic example of only focusing on behavior and skipping emotional attunement.

As a result of this episode, Mr. Tom engaged in extensive work with the whole class (as well as staff training) regarding the ownership of emotions, choices, and consequences. Gabe began to make significant progress. However, a few weeks later, Gabe decided to avoid his classwork during independent time. Mr. Tom reminded Gabe that he had a choice to complete it during the allotted independent time or during recess. Gabe continued not to do his work and read instead. At recess,

Gabe came into the classroom upset that he had to do his work. He had another meltdown, was angry, and began to swear.

Having learned more about emotional attunement, Mr. Tom decided to mirror Gabe's emotions: "You are allowed to be upset," he calmly responded. "All feelings are OK. But you are not allowed to behave that way in the classroom. If you continue doing this you will have to go to the BD classroom." As Gabe sat back down, he looked at the teacher. "Don't you want me to get over being mad?" he asked. Gabe had had an *aha* moment! He'd learned it was not acceptable to be mad from other adults, and because he felt angry and wanted to be heard, he would escalate it into a power struggle. Usually, this resulted in heightened outbursts and sometimes violence. In this case, however, Mr. Tom had created the space for Gabe to be angry, and had even validated the feeling. Something shifted. Gabe de-escalated much more quickly, moved through his emotion in about ten minutes, apologized for what he said, and began his schoolwork.

According to Sarah, "So many times as teachers we think 'teacher authority' means that all kids behave, and when they don't, we take it personally. We measure our effectiveness based on emotions: if students are happy, we are doing our job correctly. Unfortunately, this is not realistic."

Kids, just like adults, have emotions throughout the day. The emotions are not the problem; it's how we react to them. Teacher authority is a mutual respect—allowing feelings, safe boundaries, and students to know expectations and accountability measures. In this case, Gabe received all the ingredients, and they helped him move through his emotions and regulate himself more quickly than he did at the beginning of the year. Mr. Tom had validated the feeling, but invalidated the unsafe behaviors. For behavioral boundaries to be effective, emotional attunement comes first, then accountability, and then safety. Mr. Tom saw Gabe's meltdowns go from two hours to mere minutes as Gabe learned to self-regulate, refocus, and move on with the next subject. I've heard these results over and over again from parents and teachers: kids and students recover much more quickly from emotional meltdowns when using these four ingredients.

———

ONE OF THE greatest areas of struggle I see as a parenting coach is adults' inability to hold consistent behavioral boundaries. Kids learn the "loopholes" and the ways to manipulate boundaries, and test their parents. Or they develop deft verbal abilities to negotiate and argue their case. Schools overall tend to be more focused than homes on structure, rules, boundaries, consistency, and accountability. Many schools even have built-in points, fake money, or similar systems for daily behavioral management and accountability in the classroom. These important measures help schools to be a safe, predictable place for kids to attend every day. Yet, too many teachers struggle with being effective and consistent, as their own human emotions are triggered and they're pulled into power struggles that aren't productive for their own or their students' wellbeing.

Krista, a TA, worked one-on-one with students who struggled behaviorally or academically in math. April, a third-grader, was a tough cookie and wanted to do anything but math. Krista, feeling responsible, tried to "coax" her.

"Don't you like shopping, April? Let's pretend these numbers are the number of dresses."

"That's stupid."

"OK. What if we play a math game, instead?" Krista asked.

April ignored her and asked to go to the bathroom for the second time.

After April came back, she passively played the board game with constant, inappropriate jokes and laughs while Krista continued to try to engage April in math.

April could reject Krista and her ideas at a whim. This is a classic example of a teacher trying all her magic and still getting caught in the power struggle. Krista had ceded some of her authority, and April had grabbed it. There was a tug of war. Krista was now sweating, and April to a degree was in control.

TEACHER AUTHORITY

Even within the structure and boundaries of a school, if a teacher does not have personal authority, kids can chip away at the adult to try to gain some power. In my experience, kids with behavioral struggles may look to gain power or attention negatively, because they're not getting power and attention in the more positive ways that adults would like: good grades, playing sports, hard work, following the rules, and so on. It's not as if April is saying to herself, *I'm not getting attention for As and following the rules, so I'll get attention by acting out.* But as we all know from the media (whether positive or negative), "all press is good press," attention is attention. So, April is unconsciously vying for power and attention, even if through defiance.

Krista herself is likewise caught in this dynamic because she feels responsible for April's learning. Whether she's aware of it or not, Krista is backpedaling on expectations and tiptoeing around April's moodiness and defiance. April likes this because she's the one cracking jokes and showing disrespect and seems to be getting away with it. Taking responsibility for April's learning is exactly where Krista is stuck. Krista is not responsible for April's learning, but she *is* responsible for the rules and boundaries of her classroom. April is responsible for her own learning. This can be tricky territory. Certainly, a teacher plays a major role in any child's learning, but if April gets an A, it's *her* A, and if she gets a D, that's her grade as well. In short, kids are responsible for their own successes and failures, whereas teachers are responsible for holding boundaries and being creative and dynamic in their teaching. A teacher can't force the material on kids; they must be open to learning.

As with the pattern of parents' power struggles with their children, teachers can get hooked into power plays with students. What is missing in this dynamic is ownership: both adult and child are trying to get something from the other. In Krista's case, it's engagement; in April's, power. Ownership is when you let go of the other and focus on what is within your control. Krista can focus on her authority and establish the rules and boundaries of her classroom; April can choose to engage or not—that is within her power. I have seen specialists and BD teachers spend many class periods simply establishing norms, before any academic learning takes place, because some students put so much energy into testing boundaries.

HOW TO AVOID A POWER STRUGGLE

Never let them see you sweat

If you are emotionally triggered or frustrated by a student, you should excuse yourself and do what you need to do to become emotionally regulated. (Teachers have to be self-aware enough to do this.) Many teachers have said some version of, *Enough! You guys aren't listening and it's frustrating me.* It may not be visible, but you feel worked up. It's important to own whatever you feel, rather than saying your student caused you to feel this way because he or she is difficult. Your feeling is still *your* feeling; it's no one else's fault or responsibility. Take some mindful breaths, do a breathing round of a four-count breaths in, hold for four, and exhale for four. Repeat four times.

Don't work harder than your student

This statement may sound like another impossible request, because teachers are supposed to work hard on behalf of their students. Certainly, good teaching involves teachers working hard to get to know their students and their learning style, to build rapport, and to teach in creative ways. But if teachers are making ninety percent of the effort and kids only ten, the result can be off-kilter and unproductive. If teachers work harder than students, they take more responsibility for the latters' learning, which can backfire. That's why it's essential to hold kids accountable, so they can take ownership. For example, you might say: "Let me know when you're ready to go over your math homework. But we can't earn points for the Friday party unless we complete this today."

Be clear on your boundaries

There'll always be some give and take with students, depending on the time of day, energy levels, classroom dynamics, and so on. But aside from these variables, clear and consistent boundaries work wonders in reducing power struggles. If a child is rude, disrespectful, or disruptive in class, a teacher has an opportunity to mirror this misbehavior and let the child know what the expectation is: "I see that students at table four have gotten off-topic with side conversations. Do any of you want to check in about what you're talking about?" One student replies with a quick, *No.* "OK," the teacher continues. "Let's get back on topic then. Thanks!"

Power poses

Substantial research now suggests that how we hold ourselves physically conveys our own power and internal authority. This isn't about dominance; it's more about being clear and firm with students and others so that our verbal communication matches our nonverbal messaging. For example, a teacher who wants to redirect her class has more authority standing in front of the students with an open body language than she does sitting behind her desk in the corner. Harvard researcher Amy Cuddy has a great TED talk on "power poses" and how they're essential when kids want to pull you into a power struggle. With a defiant youngster, taking up space with your body—standing up, legs slightly apart, maybe even with arms out—can help. For a more timid student, who shuts down, you may want to sit on the ground and get lower than the student to show receptivity and lack of a threat.

Use the language of choice

Essential to the effectiveness of holding behavioral boundaries is using the language of choice. Some teachers may exude too much authority and be intimidating. Language that comes across as controlling ("You have to do this") can be the perfect challenge for some kids to say, "No. I don't." You may think you are in your authority, but, before you know it, you're actually in another power struggle. A way to circumvent this situation is to let kids know there are boundaries and expectations, but that they always have a choice with their behavior. They can choose to follow the expectation or not, and as such will face the corresponding consequences for those choices, positive or negative. Such an approach allows teachers to be more "hands off" in whether they have to get a child to do something. So, rather than using controlling language, a teacher can say instead: "The expectation is that you take your vocabulary test. If you choose not to take the test, that will be an incompletion, which will be factored into your grade. You may want to think about that choice and the consequence and see if that is a good choice for you." This is non-threatening language, and it takes the teacher or adult out of the equation, leaving the choice and consequence on the student's lap. This is an excellent way to circumvent a power struggle. It also can encourage critical thinking and even maturation on the student's part.

HOLDING STUDENTS ACCOUNTABLE

The pendulum has swung from more authoritarian childrearing and teaching to more permissive childrearing and teaching. When I was a student at Middlebury College in the 1990s, teachers seemed to take pride in how many books per week we had to read and the number of ten-page papers we had to write. I recall a ruthless consequence system that meant I once received no credit (essentially an F) for a paper because I dropped it electronically in the wrong place on the new online server at the time. I also remember once logging forty hours on a midterm project, and I still received a C.

In 2012, I returned to Middlebury to teach a winter-term class. Although the school was still academically challenging, I noticed the tone had changed. Professors and deans gave an exceptional amount of warning on student stress levels. I remember thinking, *What about the stress levels when I was a student?* In my class, it seemed as though many of the twenty-three students had a reason why they couldn't complete their paper on time, or had an absence or other expectations that weren't met. As a brand-new guest teacher, I wasn't sure how accommodating or strict I should be. However, picking up on the softer ethos on campus, I was quite lenient.

This shift I noticed at Middlebury reflects the larger one in parenting trends that has impacted schools and teaching. We've become more "child-centered." We think loosening expectations and deadlines and making assignments more flexible addresses the stress or mental-health issues. Instead, these measures are reactive and fear-based. We're afraid to place stress on kids, and so we backpedal. With the rise of anxiety disorders, depression, and other mental-health struggles, we've fallen into the trap of giving up boundaries and structure, thinking this will help. Making rules less rigid, however, *creates* more uncertainty and unpredictability. Anxiety is always reduced when there's more predictability, structure, and certainty in a classroom—more black and white.

In short, this pendulum has swung too far from more authoritarian approaches. It needs to return to the middle. With the crumbling of teacher authority, students have succeeded in finding loopholes, blaming adults, and getting their parents' sympathy. With the lack of accountability taught in homes and schools, children's sense of entitlement is on the rise.

We don't want to return to harsh and punitive methods for disciplining children. Principals and teachers don't want to power-trip anymore; they want to be relational with students. Yet relationality doesn't mean removing boundaries or accountability. The rigors of Middlebury didn't harm me, but I could have benefitted from a more relational dynamic. What I found in the wilderness is the perfect blend of high expectations and deep attunement to students' emotions, needs, and seeing the whole child. It's not either/or; it's both/and.

HIGH EXPECTATIONS AND HIGH ATTUNEMENT

When teachers take into account a student's whole self—their emotional *and* learning needs—they can then hold them to a high standard. When classrooms become safe places for all emotions *and* struggle, there's no need to back away from any expectation. Student resourcefulness, creativity, and grit can thrive in a supportive place—one where students are seen, heard, valued, and held accountable.

I witnessed this truth over and over again in the wilderness, where kids had to complete challenging outdoor and therapeutic curricula. Whether they were making a primitive bow-drill fire with only sticks and cordage or writing an accountability letter to their parents about the lies they had told at home, the kids' learning seemed to come from a very tough place where the children didn't believe they could do something. However, we instructors *never* changed the expectations. It might take a child a week or two longer to complete a task than intended, but we were patient. We believed each student capable of what we asked. When kids know there is no exit, they actually work hard. This is the source of happiness, esteem, and confidence.

Teachers don't need to ask kids to do less so we don't upset them, or be overly flexible about deadlines or time limits. Instead, we can instill a belief in their capabilities and start getting more comfortable with their struggling. Teachers can say *Yes* to behavioral and learning expectations <u>and</u> *Yes* to feelings and struggles:

- *The way it used to be: Yes and No.* Most teachers today grew up in classrooms that had high behavioral and learning expectations and low attunement to students' emotional needs. Kids that didn't succeed in traditional ways were made to feel dumb, or they didn't like school. This scenario is only focused on learning and doesn't take into consideration the child's emotional needs or whole self.

- *The way it is now: No and Yes.* Expectations have been loosened, and there's pressure on teachers not to give homework, or to provide extra time on tests, or to allow kids to hand in work late. More emphasis is placed on kids being happy, unstressed, and not upset. This is a fear-based approach, worried about kids' negative response to school. If teachers only give As and Bs because we want kids to "feel good," then we are catering to their emotional needs and not their learning needs.

- *The new way: Yes and Yes.* Teachers can hold high expectations with students where they challenge them academically, and allow them to struggle and feel. When there's no fear, everything's OK: success and failure. This is the true growth mindset, because everything is part of the learning, whatever grade a student gets. This mindset is also the best preparation for high school, college, and beyond because the adult world doesn't care if you "feel good." It only cares if you show up for work or pay your bills or pick your child up from school on time. When we frame safe struggle as essential to learning, we're helping kids build skills for the real world.

ACCOUNTABILITY MEASURES

As a wilderness instructor and now parent coach, I've learned that rules mean nothing without accountability measures. Lots of parents have rules and expectations, but kids learn quickly if they need to follow them. Today, we've backed away from discipline and accountability in schools and homes because we don't want to upset kids or have a power-trip as adults. But getting rid of discipline and punishments doesn't mean we need to get rid of accountability. They are different.

	PUNITIVE MEASURES	ACCOUNTABILITY MEASURES
Example	Going to detention on Saturday mornings	Losing points for the monthly class party
Targeting	The student	The student's behavior
Message	"You are bad."	"You made a bad choice."
Intent	Suffering to create change	Enforcing a rule or holding accountable
Outcome	A student feeling angry or bad	A student losing a small privilege
Long term	Shaming	De-shaming

A good example of this in the real world is speed limits. Speed limits are intended to create safety on the roads. If speed limits weren't enforced, it wouldn't feel as safe to be on the roads and highways. The rule helps to create more safety and order, just like the rules in a school. However, when you get pulled over for speeding, the message is not that you are a bad person or even a bad driver. The message is about the behavior: "Slow down! You were going too fast." This is the difference between a punitive and an accountability measure. The latter consists usually of a warning or ticket, and then you're back on the road. Does this approach change drivers' behaviors? For some, yes; for others, no. But either way, the goal is not to change behavior; the goal is to have safe roads or a safe school. Speed limits achieve this. The same is true for schools and teachers. Teachers don't intend to change one student, but rather to uphold the safety of the school.

Many parents tell me that "consequences don't work," meaning their child's behavior didn't change when they gave a consequence. But parents are focused more on the child's changing and less on upholding a household rule. I believe we need to step away from the idea of control or changing behavior and embrace the idea of holding kids to rules for safety and order.

Many kids are shockingly disrespectful to their parents today because parents feel they don't know how to change the behavior and so tolerate or accept that disrespect on some level. However, I believe parents can make a shift if they focus more on upholding respect, rather than on changing their child. One response might go as follows: "You are allowed to be upset with me. But if you make the choice to be disrespectful, you'll lose your weekend social privileges, because it is not OK to be rude to me and then go out with your friends."

Some kids receive the same consequence over and over, just like some drivers get a lot of speeding tickets. But that doesn't mean we should simply abandon consequences. That would be like saying, "Well, that driver already has ten speeding tickets. I guess they don't work with him, so we won't pull him over anymore." Consequences compound in the real world.

If the intention is to create safety and order in the classroom, teachers need to have accountability measures for students, such as a loss of privileges or points or maybe community service. I really don't think it matters if a teacher's measure changes a behavior. What matters more is upholding the container of the classroom to the benefit of all students. This in turn will teach accountability. Our actions have consequences, and certainly this lesson will be mirrored when kids are in the real world, where adults face consequences on every corner.

In summary, we don't have to throw the baby out with the bathwater. We don't have to get rid of all consequences or accountability measures because we don't want to be punitive. How can we hold boundaries in a way that is de-shaming and non-reactive? Can the intention of accountability measures promote learning? Can facing consequences be normalized as an important way to learn and know that we are all good and capable of making mistakes or unproductive choices? If we focus on the students' choices or behaviors being the issue, not on who the students are, then facing an accountability measure is just something to keep kids on their toes and invested in their learning and growing.

THE STORY OF APRIL

How could Krista have had a new outcome with April, where Krista stayed in her teacher authority, sidestepped the power struggle, and held April accountable for her learning? Let's rerun the scenario.

"Hi, April! Today you need to take a math quiz."

"That is stupid. Why would I want to do that?"

"OK. Well, you certainly may choose not to like it, and you may even find it stupid. I'm OK with that. Not everybody likes math. However, it's still the expectation of this class period. Please pull out your pencil."

April glances up and Krista wonders what her next move should be. April decides to push a little. "What if I don't want to take the stupid test?"

Krista calmly composes herself. "That is entirely your choice. Your schoolwork is up to you. But I think you know the consequence if you choose not to take the test. You will work with me more one-on-one, and you'll not gain points to return to the classroom with your peers. Let me know your choice. If you finish before the class ends and we have time, I say we have another round of Uno."

April raises her eyes as though she's contemplating her choice. She then picks up her pencil and begins to take her test. She remains focused until she completes it, getting stuck on a few questions but sticking with it. Then, she puts her pencil down, and a big smile breaks across her face. Jenna looks at the clock and pulls out the Uno cards, and the two settle into another round of a long-standing competition. Krista successfully held April accountable and gave nothing for April to power-struggle against.

chapter 5

INGREDIENT #3—VALUING STRUGGLE

Struggle Is Where All Learning Happens

🌿 **SARAH WRITES:** Prior to my son's learning to control himself, I was in a constant battle with him about homework. Although I am a teacher who advocates constantly that kids should struggle through their own work, I wasn't following my own advice at home . . . until recently. Over the summer, my son was required to do at least an hour a day of academics to prevent him from falling behind at school. We'd been working on telling time with a clock. At this point, he was learning quickly and seemed confident. On one particular day, we sat down, and I showed him some times; he called them out with a proud smile on his face. When I displayed the final time on the clock, however, everything changed. My son completely shut down and had tears in his eyes and refused to answer. I was shocked because he'd been doing so well, and I was unsure why he was so upset. I immediately felt the urge to rescue him.

My natural instinct was to ask him what was wrong and try to convince him that he could do it, to tell him it was the last one—to try to cheer him up. But because of what I was learning, I knew that soothing words were not what he wanted to hear and would most likely make the situation worse. So, I created space. "It seems like you might be upset,"

I said. "Let me know when you're ready to talk about it." He initially refused and stayed in shut-down mode. I told him that when he was ready to talk, I'd be ready to listen. Less than two minutes later, my son came to me and told me he didn't know which number to pick if the shorter hand was between two numbers. I realized at that moment that I'd unknowingly emphasized being correct and praising him for a quick answer at the expense of valuing struggle in learning. This focus on getting the "right" answer resulted in him shutting down, because he was unsure. I hadn't created an emotionally safe environment for him to be in a place of struggle or not knowing.

In our society, we tend to value the correct answer and not the struggle, and as teachers we do this constantly. We're proud when students get the question right; it means we've taught them well and they understand the material. We're conditioned to respond to correct answers instead of helping students think through something, solve a problem, or develop skills when they don't know what to do. Always looking for the right answers prevents us from enduring through hard times. If we can reframe struggle as an important part of learning—one that includes *all* aspects of learning, right answers and wrong—then we'll be building emotionally resilient students.

After my son and I talked about how to address the fact that the shorter hand was between two numbers, we also had a conversation about what to do the next time he didn't know the answer. We talked about how it was OK to not know something. He could either say he didn't know or ask to take a break and come back and ask questions. I wanted to reframe the discussion so he'd understand it was acceptable to be curious about the material, instead of thinking only in terms of correct and incorrect. This is how we develop the growth mindset. It provides a safe space to struggle and develop skills to persevere.

Though parents and teachers may not be able to prevent all meltdowns, I believe kids' emotional reactivity to learning can be dramatically reduced when struggle is framed as normal and even good. When we allow our students to sit with what they're feeling, when we create space, they're able to move through the emotions and develop endurance. The more we try to prevent, fix, or push emotions away, the more students lose the ability to persevere. Teachers are modeling all the time, so if teachers reject struggle, students will also. Conversely, when teachers welcome struggle, students are more likely to embrace their struggles.

The less teachers focus on the right answer, the more students will detach from the idea that they always need to be correct. Teachers could employ responses such as, "What thinking did you use to come up with that answer?" or "That is interesting," "Tell me more," or "Are there any other answers or strategies you see?" Collaborative problem-solving encourages critical thinking and engaged learning, rather than a focus on being right or wrong. ❧

BOULDERS ON THE TRAIL

KRISSY WRITES: We all have our own life-trail, littered with different rocks and boulders that we have to work around or surmount. Hovering parents and teachers can get caught trying to roll these obstacles off their child's path, so his or her life is smooth and relatively free of difficulties. Whether the child is having problems with their friend, or finding schoolwork hard, or is undergoing emotional or behavioral challenges, many adults intervene in the backbreaking work of clearing the way. This approach isn't sustainable, as around every bend in the trail are more rocks and boulders, maybe even some cliffs that need to be scaled.

In my wilderness work and parent coaching I observed that many kids are passive when it comes to life's problems and expect someone else to fix them. To use the same metaphor, it's almost as if kids sit down in front of the boulder and wait for someone to move it. As a result, they're not building the skills necessary to get up and over the rocks. In the wilderness, it was clear that no one would do for a student what a student could do for him- or herself. So, kids learned that unless they tried to figure out their path, they'd be sitting on the trail for a long time. This assumption of responsibility led students to face their problems—a wonderful process to watch. This could only happen when kids owned and reframed their struggle as positive, even beneficial.

Children today aren't being taught that the rocks and boulders in their life are actually opportunities. Every struggle offers a lesson, or it develops a skill for facing something coming around the bend in the trail. For example, being rejected socially in sixth grade might be an important primer for high school. But contemporary adults don't tend to look at such occurrences this way; we tend to feel bad for the child left out. Ancient cultures designed "rites of passage" meant to put young people in a place of struggle, where they could grow and mature. What if we reframed middle-school and high-school difficulties this way?

The same applies to the classroom. If a student is confronted with an obstacle, teachers can frame the situation as an important moment for learning: to turn a thorny problem into an empowering life opportunity.

SOCIAL EXCLUSION

Jessa happened to land in a challenging social environment in junior high. Three different middle schools were merging into one regional junior high and high school, thus bringing lots of different groups together. Jessa's best friend, Maddie, had some other close friends she knew from her gymnastics team coming to their same school. Maddie was ecstatic, but Jessa was worried. As it turned out, Jessa's fears materialized in front of her eyes. This new group wanted Maddie with them and seemed threatened by any of Maddie's other friends. They put pressure on Maddie to reject Jessa, and sadly Maddie chose her gymnastics friends. Jessa found herself in a spiral of anxiety adjusting to all the changes of junior high as well as the exclusion of a big group of popular girls. She came home crying every night. Maddie wouldn't even look at her anymore, and Jessa was completely ignored socially.

Luckily, Jessa's teacher, Mrs. P., was attuned to her and saw she seemed down. However, Mrs. P. missed the social dynamics. Subtle bullying is so tricky because it isn't obvious to adults; girls, in particular, can act pleasantly in front of teachers and be mean when no teacher is around. Jessa appreciated Mrs. P.'s interest but didn't want to rat out Maddie, as she'd then never be able to enter the group. Mrs. P. wasn't satisfied with Jessa's vague answer about why she was struggling and so she asked the guidance counselor, Sally, to check in on Jessa.

In their first meeting, Jessa felt safe enough to tell Sally the whole story: in fact, she blurted it out between her tears. Since Sally had been trained in Brave Teaching and a growth mindset, she decided to take a new approach with Jessa. Although Sally regularly held group discussions on friendships and bullying with the middle-school and junior-high girls, she knew it was hard to confront social exclusion, because it's so nuanced and largely hidden from teachers and adults. The girls could deny that anything was wrong and then perhaps be even crueler to the victim behind the adults' backs. Sally also knew she had even less ability to monitor and regulate how kids grouped together outside of school. Therefore, instead of trying to change the girls' behavior, Sally decided to work one-on-one with Jessa, framing the struggle as a "boulder" on Jessa's trail.

"You know, Jessa," Sally said. "It might seem like you are a victim and there's nothing else to do except suffer in this situation. But what if I told you that girls use social exclusion in high school, college, and even as adults? Every girl and woman faces this obstacle at some point in her life; it just happens to be in your way right now. I want you to know that it's not personal; in fact, it's universal. What if you saw this as an important rock to climb over on your life-trail? What if you could learn this important lesson before high school? Although this situation is painful and uncomfortable, what if you framed it as an opportunity?"

"What do you mean?" Jessa replied incredulously, as she wiped away tears. "What do you suggest?"

"Well, I don't have an exact answer: I thought perhaps you could be in charge of problem-solving it. I do have one suggestion, however.

What if you become like a scientist and experimented with different approaches with the girls each day, and you took notes? For example, you could ignore them, or be friendly, or make new friends, or act like it doesn't bother you, and so on. Whatever happened, you could just keep gathering data, and then we'd talk the following week."

Jessa nodded, thanked Sally, and returned to class. She wasn't sure what to think, but she noticed she was less unhappy. She now had a strategy and felt more empowered. She would try new approaches and also be an observer. She would watch the dynamics. She would be curious. She would find the important lesson.

After a few months of working with Sally, Jessa noted some changes. First, when Jessa no longer cared about being excluded, things began to shift. She saw that the best approach was to be friendly and detached from the outcome of joining Maddie's gang. Jessa decided not to pick a social group, but to float around different clusters and be friendly with everyone. Jessa also observed that she didn't take these groups' behavior so personally and began to see how the girls in the group were mean to one another, and not just outsiders. In fact, Jessa could see that although Maddie put on a smile, at times she was herself excluded from an inner circle of three in the group. It seemed as if these girls controlled Maddie. Jessa felt sorry for Maddie. Rather than trying to get herself into the group or force Maddie out, Jessa made sure to be nice to Maddie every day. That weekend, Maddie invited her to go to a movie, and Jessa continued to be friendly without any expectations. This worked and they had a great time.

Slowly, Jessa began to feel grateful for not being confined to one group. She knew that belonging to this popular group would mean being loyal and eating lunch with them every day. There were times she wished she could belong to the group, but she also started to see its downsides. Jessa told Sally she was learning the important lesson of social exclusion, and felt she was climbing over the boulder and growing emotionally. She noticed she was getting invited to more gatherings. She had joined after-school clubs, had started basketball, and was auditioning for the school play. Jessa felt empowered and even grateful for having undergone social exclusion.

Jessa's growth and maturation would have been less likely had Mrs. P. not been attuned and Sally not reframed struggle as an opportunity. Critically, Sally "normalized" or "depersonalized" the struggle. So often, children today feel that something is wrong with them when they struggle or feel unhappy, when in fact what happened to Jessa was perhaps one of the most common experiences of childhood. This reframing and small, simple shifts can reduce stress and suffering in a student, build resiliency, and promote social and emotional learning. By working with her teacher and guidance counselor rather than feeling like a victim of social exclusion and subtle bullying, Jessa refashioned difficulty as a life opportunity. In this way, schools can be places of internal skill-development by bringing in the four essential ingredients.

JAMES'S STORY

James was a highly creative and extremely gifted sixteen-year-old who played the piano at a conservatory in New York City at the college level. The problem was that he didn't want to play the piano anymore. His mother, Rebecca, was the epitome of a stage mom—directing and managing James constantly, doing her best to keep him on task. James had executive-functioning issues and anxiety. Because of Rebecca's dominant personality, James became very passive. He also began to isolate himself and avoid school at times in an attempt to manage his sense of being overwhelmed. This was a disaster for Rebecca.

Rebecca admitted to me that she'd managed James since he was a little boy. She told me she'd seen his musical talents *and* his lack of organization, and so had stepped in. It was clear to me that, as she stepped in, he stepped away. After many years of being stuck and James spiraling downward, Rebecca realized she needed to step away, so James could step in. With lots of parent coaching, Rebecca identified that she had only two real rules: follow curfew and no drugs (James had been caught smoking pot). Rebecca was going to hold him accountable for those two rules and leave the rest to him. This was very hard for her, but she knew the status quo wasn't working. So, she took a risk.

The first few months of this strategy were awful, as James was frequently late for school (Rebecca no longer got him up in the morning). James didn't do his homework and also stopped playing the piano. Over time, however, new practices emerged. James began teaching piano lessons at school to younger kids. He liked playing music in a less competitive environment, and teaching younger children reflected this. He also earned accolades in a painting class, and, without Rebecca's knowledge, began looking at colleges. He called his therapist for appointments, as he realized he needed help with his executive-functioning and anxiety issues. He was in the school play, as he was so natural and gifted. He even texted his mother to see if she wanted to go out for lunch. This was all a shock to Rebecca: although she still wanted to control and direct James, she learned to stop herself.

What became evident was that Rebecca was taking James down a very narrow path (school, piano) that was really *her* path. As James began to take full ownership of his obstacles and life-path he realized he hated the highly competitive world of conservatories and started to explore more arts: plays, sculpture, comedy, and writing. He stepped into who he really was. When it came time to write his college essay (for liberal arts and not a music school), one college president even wrote him back because he was so impressed by his writing and essay. In parenting and in teaching, we have to let go and let kids take ownership: this is where the true magic happens.

Ownership, the basis of the Four Ingredients, includes emotions, behaviors, and also one's problems. In addition to the ownership of emotions and behaviors if a student acts out, it's necessary to make explicit the ownership of problems. Adults, of course, play a key role in providing support for students' problems, but if a student doesn't take ownership of a problem (as was the case with James' executive functioning), it's unlikely the problem will be solved.

MAX'S STORY

Max is a second-grade student who has to see the reading specialist weekly, where he's being given extra reading assignments. Yet, if Max doesn't own this problem, and instead sees it as a blow against his self-esteem, he may barely engage with the tutor and avoid the extra weekly assignments. Teachers, the tutor, and the parents may all own the problem, instead of Max.

With skill-development around ownership and problem-solving, Max can learn to reframe this obstacle as an opportunity. These skills give Max a "trail map" for how to move forward. Everyone has different obstacles in life; this one happens to be on Max's trail. A reading delay doesn't need to weigh on a student's self-esteem. With active participation and ownership, Max can turn this negative into an empowering reframe. Learning to climb over this boulder could be an incredible asset for his future education. I witnessed this process again and again in the wilderness, where students developed skills, took ownership of their life problems, faced them head-on, and moved forward. It's time to bring these critical skills into the school system.

SAFE STRUGGLE VERSUS UNSAFE STRUGGLE

Before teachers and schools can really let kids struggle, it's essential to determine if the struggle is safe. *Safe* social exclusion is when a child is not invited to a weekend party; this happens probably every weekend somewhere. *Unsafe* social exclusion might involve humiliation on social media. Of course, determining what's safe or unsafe isn't an exact science, and there are gray areas. However, it's precisely this inexactitude that requires teachers, parents, and other adults to *lean in* to observe and be aware of what is happening in kids' lives.

We've already seen how most parents think *all* struggle is unsafe. What we're talking about instead is what I call "safe struggle." I tell parents that safe struggle is if their children are finding things difficult

with friends, chores, rules, sibling relationships, respectful communication, homework, tech limits, and so on. These daily challenges, though
unpleasant, give lots of opportunity for skill-development and essential
maturation.

The classroom also offers plenty of examples of safe struggles: peer
conflicts, inability to concentrate, homework challenges, following
the rules, friend dynamics, respecting the teacher, completing tasks,
classroom chores. Many teachers are annoyed when things don't run
smoothly, but the daily hiccup is exactly where skill-development happens. For example, a student could cultivate patience when a field-trip
is canceled, develop problem-solving skills after a conflict at recess, or
learn collaboration when working together to complete a classroom
assignment.

Before "fixing" a situation, teachers should ask themselves, "Is this
safe or unsafe struggle?" Is it safe for your student to find it hard to tell
the time? It is safe for him or her to find social interactions awkward?
Is it safe for a child to become frustrated about homework? Is it safe for
a child to be anxious about tests? Obviously, I think it is.

That said, parents, teachers, or principals must interrupt any
struggle they deem unsafe. Bullying; physical, verbal, or emotional
abuse; cheating, lying, peer pressure, and substance abuse all fall
under the heading of UNSAFE. Teachers also need to assess unsafe
struggle in the context of whether the student needs more services or
support: for instance, a guidance counselor, an IEP, a math tutor, or
a reading program. However, if teachers determine that a struggle is
safe, it's my belief they should let go and allow kids to wrestle with
the situation.

PROBLEM-SOLVING SKILLS

In schools, the notion of problem-solving arises mostly in math class.
I believe this is limited: we can't allow kids only to solve problems in
math, but then intervene with problems in their lives. Young adults

are leaving for college or the real world without experience of being resourceful and navigating their own problems. Certainly, the omnipresence of smartphones means that instead of dealing with something independently, kids text their parents their problems. Parents reinforce the behavior by being on standby to run interference at a moment's notice. One of my constant refrains when I coach is to tell parents not to offer a solution unless their child specifically asks, "Mom, what should I do?" Kids will tell their parents a problem, such as being excluded by a friend, and before the story is over the parent has already given advice. As parents, we can do a much better job of waiting, listening, and being empathic, but refraining from action unless solicited.

As a parent, I have a lot of instant solutions to fix and manage my kids' lives. My learning edge—the point where I have most to learn and find it hardest to adjust—is to hold my tongue and listen, and refrain from automatic responses. Although it's become a more normal reply, when I first started offering this response to my daughter ("You know, you're really good at problem-solving. I'm going to let you be in charge of the problem and solve it yourself. I'm happy to listen and support you, but I want you to be in charge of it"), she'd pause a minute, look at me sideways, and then break out in a smile and wander off. The wheels were turning in her head. Shortly, I'd hear back from her about her solution. Other times, my kids would say, "*I don't know!*" And I'd say, "Well, sleep on it. Maybe something will come to you tomorrow." Sure enough, something did.

We're robbing our kids of their learning when we always jump in with a quick fix. It's true that my girls get annoyed with this response, too. But they've matured emotionally and have become quite independent problem-solvers, whether they like how I frame the situation or not.

Schools and the classroom also offer valuable sites for reframing. Sarah Love treats every problem, conflict, or situation at school as an opportunity for a child to develop resiliency and skills. The underlying message of this response is *I believe you are capable.* Is there any better message we can instill in students today? When we value struggle, when we frame obstacles as opportunities for growth, let boulders stay on children's trails and encourage them to figure out what to do with them, we set the tone for lifelong learning and developing a true growth mindset.

chapter 6

INGREDIENT #4—SAFETY

Creating an Emotionally Safe Environment

AN ENVIRONMENT WHERE students are independent learners and owners of everything they think, say, do, and feel comes from the teacher setting the tone. Of paramount importance in teaching these skills is that the classroom must feel emotionally safe. An emotionally safe environment is one where all feelings are welcome, respected, and valued; where kids don't need to hide who they are, escalate behaviorally, or blame others. Instead, students are welcome to feel and sit with their emotions and to share them if they are comfortable.

To teach emotional resilience and ownership in her fourth-grade classroom, Sarah Love designed promises with her students (for older grades you can call them "classroom agreements"). These involved measures ensuring structure, transitions, and accountability before students were expected to master new skills.

🖌 **SARAH WRITES:** When I plan out my first six weeks of school, I'm very strategic with how I set up and run my classroom and integrate the teaching of these resiliency skills. The internal skills can be taught in the context of other learning, which is helpful so you don't fall behind teaching academics. Ownership, accountability, and self-regulation can be embedded in classwork.

In the first week of school, I develop management and procedures in the classroom itself. I've found that when you allow students into the process, they gain ownership and are willing to follow the expectations, as opposed to feeling controlled and dictated to. Each year's norms and promises change, depending on the classroom (this year, for instance, my students wanted to be more responsible). However that procedure is structured, you'll be surprised at what your students come up with.

Our classroom norms and promises this year were as follows:

CLASSROOM AGREEMENTS

1) *Create a schema with the class.* Have conversations about what worked well and what students want to do differently from the previous year. Teachers should reframe negative feedback as a positive. The purpose of this exercise isn't to blame the previous teacher, but for students to discuss the past school year themselves and come up with things that did or didn't work for them.

2) *Set the tone* that this year students will be responsible for everything they think, do, and feel. When confronted with a disagreement or problem, students aren't allowed to talk about what the other student did. First, they have to talk about what *they* felt and thought, and how *they* responded to a situation.

3) *Students are allowed to feel upset or mad* in the classroom, but they are *not* allowed to behave angrily or act out their feelings.

4) *Students have choices.* They have the choice to talk or not talk about their feelings.

5) *Accountability.* If a student chooses to act out an emotion through an inappropriate behavior, the student will be held accountable.

We wrote these norms and promises on chart paper, and each student signed it. I would love to report that, thenceforth, the students responded immediately. But they didn't, and they won't in your class. Some students will fall in love with the rules, and you'll enjoy a honeymoon period; others will test the promises. These are all normal responses and to be expected. To prevent losing the skills you've built already, it's important to remain consistent and genuine.

Jennifer is an excellent student: she completes assignments, understands quickly, and always participates in class discussions. She seems to be every teacher's dream, except she struggles emotionally and doesn't want to take responsibility for her feelings or behavior. Used to receiving only positive attention and unable to receive constructive criticism easily, she nonetheless appears to have excellent executive-functioning and good leadership skills. However, she still expects the teacher to fix every problem and is very quick to assign blame.

Many of us have had students like Jennifer. At the beginning of the year, I noticed that every time Jennifer encountered a problem, whether socially or academically, she wanted me to fix it, and there was an explosion of emotions. If I gave her an answer or told her what to do, she'd immediately use it to fix the problem, and become happy. However, even though Jennifer soaked up all my lessons about responsibility, allowing emotions to flow, and creating classroom norms, she still found things difficult.

One day, Jennifer approached me after lunch extremely upset. I asked her if she'd like to talk, and she completely unraveled, telling me how she'd brought a dollar to lunch and was playing with it at recess when another student ran up to her and tore it. Her emotions continued to escalate as she told the story. Instead of stepping in and telling Jennifer that I'd talk to the other student, I determined that the situation was safe and not a matter of bullying and decided to let her have this "safe struggle."

I validated how Jennifer felt and asked her what she was going to do. Jennifer's response (as it was many times from the beginning of the year) was "I don't know." I think her reply was genuine, as she'd not done a lot of her own problem-solving. I told her to consider thinking about it and that if she wanted to talk further about it, we could. This is exactly where teachers have to accept a little discomfort. So often, we want everything clear and solved; however, when we hand things over to kids we allow for a degree of uncertainty.

About twenty-five minutes later, Jennifer came to me and said she'd given the matter some thought and wanted to talk. By simply coming to me, she was showing assertiveness. Jennifer told me that she couldn't blame the other student and that she had to take responsibility for her action, which was bringing a dollar to play with at recess. She added that it might not be a good idea to bring a dollar to recess anymore. "It sounds like you used what we learned in class to solve your problem," I responded, and Jennifer smiled and walked off. In not replying, "Great job! I really like that idea," but rather identifying that the student used his or her own abilities to solve the problem, I communicate to the student that he or she is capable of solving the problem.

The most important part of developing these skills is not necessarily creating promises and norms, but accountability and follow-through. If teachers aren't consistent and don't hold students accountable to the classroom norms and promises, they'll never develop these skills. If children know there are boundaries that can be breached or there's no accountability measure, they'll never take ownership for any of their decisions, good or bad.

Accountability measures are key if you want students to become more self-reliant. Some accountability measures can be created to apply to the entire class, others will need to be individualized. These measures can be decided once problems and norms are developed. One example of an accountability measure for the whole class is that wasting time in class will result in losing recess time or a free period or another subject in order to complete the work. Another example is that not completing homework will result in a student being charged money, if you employ a banking system; if you use a fuzzy system, then students pay you an earned fuzzy. For a middle-school or high-school student, the penalty might mean going to study lunch. If a student is disrespectful to a substitute teacher, you can have the student write an email to apologize. If there's an issue with another student, you can have one student write a letter to the other. These measures aren't used as a punishment, but as a means to hold the student responsible for his or her behavior.

Every year, we create online bank accounts for our students. Money is credited to their account if they attend school, undertake classroom jobs, meet expectations, and so on. Money is debited if they don't turn in homework or fail to meet expectations. Every week, students send their parents a snapshot email of their accounts so the latter can see what is happening at school (for example, not turning in homework).

Midway through one year, after the second semester was over and report cards had been sent home, a mother (whom we'll call Miriam) emailed me upset that her daughter (whom we'll call Cheryl) wasn't completing homework. Miriam requested a meeting, during which she asked me to email what Cheryl's homework was *each day* so that Miriam knew. Miriam hadn't been looking at the snapshots Cheryl was sending her, and so missed out on holding her daughter accountable. Now Miriam was overwhelmed, upset, and wanted help, and thought my sending an email was the best way forward.

Unfortunately, Miriam's idea wouldn't have helped Cheryl's struggle to turn in homework. After talking, Miriam and I decided that Cheryl would email her homework to Miriam instead of writing it in a planner. After two days, Miriam emailed me again to tell me Cheryl was still lying about homework. Miriam wanted me once again to email her daily with the homework. I helped Miriam understand that if we did that, we'd definitely ensure that Cheryl did her homework, but the second we stopped, Cheryl would continue with the same old patterns. I encouraged Miriam to create accountability measures at home. Although Miriam wasn't thrilled about this, she checked Cheryl's bank account, held her accountable directly, and didn't allow her to go to her friend's house on the weekend. These simple measures helped turn Cheryl's behavior around. Cheryl became more honest about her homework and communicated what she needed to do each night. 🌿

YES TO FEELINGS/NO TO BEHAVIOR

KRISSY WRITES: Structure is critical to creating an emotionally safe environment, especially when disruptive behavior is in the classroom. Structure allows kids to emotionally self-regulate. By "structure," I mean a *structured response* to emotions and behavior. When teachers can say *Yes* to a child's feeling and *No* to a child's behavior, we accomplish a lot at once. We create emotional safety and accept the child and his or her emotions, and even validate the child's feelings. When we say *No* to a child's behavior, we establish classroom safety, set behavioral boundaries, and hold students accountable. Implied in this simple structured response is a choice. A structured response is, "It's OK to be anxious. That is a normal feeling to have around taking a test. It is not OK to shut down and refuse to take it. If you choose not to take the test, you'll have to take it during special time, and not academic time. You can decide what is best for you."

When we validate feelings and still hold behavioral boundaries, kids have a choice to self-regulate or not. This choice is where all maturation happens. When kids make the best choice for themselves, the blame and power struggle are removed. Certainly teachers don't give a totally free choice, but students are given the power to think through what is best rather than simply oppose and rebel. If a student chooses to be defiant, it usually means losing a privilege or something the student actually wants.

More often than not, teachers find themselves in a power struggle with their students and don't even realize how they got there, which likely can lead to an emotional conflict between teacher and student. When this happens, a teacher loses touch with his or her teacher authority. When teachers set the tone through a structured response of *yes to feelings/no to behavior*, they stay firmly in their teacher authority.

Most critically, this response actually helps kids emotionally regulate. Over and over again, I've seen kids feel validated by the *yes to feelings*, and then choose to self-regulate. At home, a child may choose to go to their room on their own and stop their disrespectful communication with a parent. In the classroom, kids can choose to stop being disruptive and rejoin class activity. By choosing and self-regulating *on their own*, kids take a gigantic leap forward in their emotional maturation.

EMOTIONALLY SAFE TEACHER RESPONSES

- "It seems like you might be frustrated. Let me know if you want to talk about it."
- "I imagine it's frustrating to get a math problem wrong that you thought you got right. I'm happy to walk through the problem with you."
- "Your feelings are important to me. I want to hear what is upsetting you. Can you take four deep breaths and then tell me?"
- "That sounds difficult. I'm going to let you be in charge of solving it. Let me know what you think is the best approach."
- "Yes, your thoughts and beliefs are valid."
- "Why don't you take some time and think about how you want to problem-solve the conflict you're having? I am available to speak with you when you are ready."

EXAMPLES OF CREATING EMOTIONAL SAFETY

1) *Institute in morning circle a feelings check.* Make a poster with faces that display various feelings and emotional states. Ask the students to scan the poster and choose a word that best fits their current feeling. At first, many kids will find this strange, but most grow to like it—especially since students aren't asked to explain their feelings. Since nobody fixes or tries to change those feelings, kids feel relieved just to share and be heard. I once performed this in a college classroom. Although

emotions were the backdrop of their lives, these students had never consciously brought attention to their emotions and strongly weighted feelings as either "happy = good" or "anxiety = bad." Simply to notice and identify their feeling without judgment was refreshing to students. Instituting a feelings check is one way to establish emotional safety in the classroom.

2) *Make a list of the unsafe behaviors.* The teacher can enumerate the following: **disrespect to the teacher or other students** (such as talking back, name-calling, defiance, and angry/snapping/inappropriate tone); **hurting others** (such as physical harm, emotional putdowns, or bullying); **lying, cheating, or stealing** (spelling out each of these items).

3) *Discuss other expectations.* In addition to unsafe behaviors, the teacher can discuss listening to whomever is talking, completing a classroom chore, keeping belongings neat, cleaning up after yourselves, staying focused on the task at hand, and so on.

4) *Establish accountability measures.* After going over these various behavioral boundaries, the teacher and class can make a list of what happens if a student crosses a behavioral boundary. This can be a collaborative process where students give input and ideas for consequences. Students are usually impressively good at identifying appropriate measures—perhaps even better than the teacher. The teacher has the final say, but listening to students' ideas helps create buy-in. Some ideas are:

- Losing the bouncy (yoga) ball for a week
- Staying in for recess at study-lunch if not paying attention or participating in classroom work
- Making a gift for a student who was teased or hurt
- Going to the principal's office if lying or cheating
- Taking a break on the "peace mat" if two students have a conflict

• Doing community service to the classroom or school if you break something

As you can see, these aren't punitive; they are measures to hold students accountable to the rules. The underlying message is: *All students are good and all feelings are OK, but we are all capable of making poor choices—and poor choices have corresponding consequences.* Interestingly, kids like these rules as they keep the classroom secure and everyone feels they are held to the same rules, which encourages a spirit of fairness and collaboration. I believe children also like to "clear the slate" when they do act out. An accountability measure like reparation of some sort helps kids recognize consequences, keep their inner integrity and esteem, lessen shaming, and move on.

5) *Problem-solve in a collaborative group.* This essential part of wilderness therapy involves the teacher/counselor asking the group to solve a particular problem together. For example, we might invite the group to come up with accountability measures for breaking rules—such as kids not listening to substitute teachers or girls splitting into social groups and excluding other girls. The open discussion of issues in a safe and emotionally attuned way helps build problem-solving skills. Because the group is responsible, students' investment in the process and in finding a solution is increased. This approach releases the idea that the teacher or adult has the answer, which is really empowering to students.

6) *Teach assertive communication skills with a focus on public speaking.* I address this more in Part 2. However, suffice to say here that assertive communication involves using the first-person singular rather than second-person singular: *I think, I feel, I believe, I want, I need, I hope, I request.* Conversely, "You" statements are passive and project blame on others. When kids state their thoughts, feelings, and needs assertively, blame is removed and effective communication established. To help build this tool, teachers can have students do short public-speaking

assignments (one to two minutes for elementary, two to five minutes for middle, and five to ten minutes for high school) around an idea or belief. This is another powerful skill to bring into the classroom and increase emotional learning.

EXAMPLES OF UNSAFE CLASSROOMS

Conversely, here are examples of *unsafe* classrooms:

1) Students undermining the teacher
2) Student bullies gaining traction in controlling the classroom
3) Students not feeling safe enough to express their thoughts, feelings, and opinions
4) Chaos and unpredictability
5) A lack of or inconsistent accountability
6) Students disengaged from their learning
7) Any response on your part that is a way to control the behavior of a student or the class for an expected response. These are empty threats and only show kids you want control. You must validate and give back the control for the students to self-regulate.

With feelings checks, behavioral boundaries with accountability measures, collaborative group problem-solving, assertive communication, and valuing struggle with the assignment of public speaking in place, the classroom becomes an emotionally safe container. This ingredient ensures that the three other essential ingredients will be effective. This is the sweet spot for teachers to aim for and where emotional growth takes off in students.

chapter 7

WORKING WITH PARENTS

❧ SARAH WRITES: I am happy to report that integrating the *Brave Parenting* philosophy into my classroom has had a significantly positive impact on my working relationships with parents. This year, I was clear with parents about my non-rescuing techniques. They were open and actually found the strategy reassuring. Complaints from parents have significantly decreased, and my parents have also felt encouraged to learn how to empower their own children.

This chapter lays out how to use these techniques with parents. The most important shift is for teachers to move from fixing to a collaborative problem-solving role with parents. As a teacher, you'll still receive various complaints, but the dynamics will change. Your teacher authority will be evident, accusatory emails will decrease, and student independence will rise.

I should note that it took me a long time to arrive at this point, so I thought I'd share with you, the reader, my learning curve with parents.

During my student-teaching years, my excellent supervising teacher told me, "If you are not ready by the time you leave, I didn't do my job." Well, she did her job. When I began actually teaching, the rush was indescribable. After a few weeks of transitioning, the class was mine. However, I discovered that teaching included dealing with parents, of which up to that point I'd had no experience. My supervising teacher came to see me and explained that I had an unhappy parent. My reaction was absolute panic: *Why were they unhappy? Was I in trouble?* I was horrified, and begged my cooperating teacher to come to the meeting so I wouldn't have to talk. She agreed, but when the parents arrived, the teacher left and was nowhere to be found. I knew she was trying to teach me a lesson, but I thought I was going to fall apart. I was alone with parents who were unhappy.

As I listened to the parents' complaints, I came to realize that although they were unhappy, and I felt their feelings were directed at me, their emotions weren't *about* me. They were worried that their child wasn't good enough. I didn't have kids at this time, but I genuinely felt empathy for them for their fears and how their extreme reaction was directed at me. We formed a plan of action, and I learned something unexpected that day: I didn't need to fear parents, but I had to listen and to understand that I was a specialist and they needed my support. Now as a parent *and* a teacher, I understand this feeling on both sides.

Unhappy parents can cause many teachers to shut down. We respond with fear and question ourselves, asking if we're good enough. But we *are* good enough. When parents react, it's because of their fear and desire to rescue their kids. As teachers, we must listen to parents' concerns but not feel responsible for their emotions. The no-rescue policy applies to students *and* parents.

As I implemented my new philosophy with my class, I also tried it with parents. Prior to this, I'd done a lot of rescuing and fixing so parents would "like me" and not complain. Usually, this only worked temporarily, if at all. When we become fixers, we assume responsibility for the problem, and parents then blame us if the outcome doesn't work for them, which creates more anger and frustration. Most teachers find this a frightening prospect. We're already under so much pressure, which is why our natural reaction to an email from an angry parent is to become defensive, get upset, worry, and shut down, or go into rescue mode. Again, this is a skills gap in kids and adults in handling emotions and conflict. Although some teachers may naturally possess these skills, none of us are taught in school to validate parents' feelings (rather than take it personally) or to work collaboratively and problem-solve together (rather than rescue and fix).

SOCIAL CONCERNS

How many teachers have received an email from a parent about their child being excluded at recess, or expressing their belief that their child is being bullied? Probably all. This generation of parents has a much different concept of what it means to be bullied than previous ones: if a child feels *any* social rejection, it's perceived to be bullying. In previous chapters, we discussed when it was appropriate to intervene and when kids should be allowed to problem-solve. Regardless, all teachers have received an email about so-called bullying. In the past I've said, "I am happy to talk with Sierra about this, and ask other kids to stop excluding her." However, this response merely creates dependency and reliance on teachers. And if the problem isn't fixed, guess who's going to be upset? That's right: the parents. So, what do teachers do? How do we respond without making the situation worse?

A girl in my class this year (let's call her Sharon) struggled with social rejection, which seemed to happen a lot because other kids were frustrated at her neediness. I received an email from her mother (whom I'll name Helen), begging for help. Helen didn't know what to do and was very worried that Sharon had no friends, a common fear for many parents. Instead of easily rescuing Helen by telling her that everything would be OK and that I'd take care of the situation, I did the opposite. I validated Helen's feelings and told her I understood. I also asked her what she'd like me to do. Helen's response was that she wanted me to fix it. Again, I resisted. What was clear to me in the classroom was that Sharon lacked problem-solving skills.

I told Helen that we needed to address Sharon's deficits in problem-solving collaboratively instead of focusing on social rejection. I reiterated that we encouraged the development of these skills at school and home through specific lessons focusing on how to sit with and accept uncomfortable feelings, and how to solve difficult situations as they arose. I made sure that Helen understood that as a class we read a tremendous number of books that contained stories of tough experiences and feelings, which helped students relate to what they might experience in their lives. When Sharon was upset, I said to Helen, I used continuous validation and reframing, which enabled her to move through hard emotions as well as understand her feelings more. Sharon and I also spent a good deal of time working on understanding perception and how perception can change based on every person's experience (more on this in Part 2). Additionally, I offered a safe space for Sharon to talk to me or seek guidance if she wanted.

Additionally, I also offered Helen some skills to work on with her daughter at home. I encouraged Helen to validate Sharon's feelings of frustration and to ask her daughter to solve problems. I encouraged Helen to offer Sharon advice only if she asked for it, and to hear her daughter out. I emphasized that Sharon's problem was not Helen's responsibility, but that Helen could be an advisor and supporter. I suggested that Helen could advise Sharon to ask new friends to play with her, or to try something different with her recent friends, and remind Sharon that in friendships she needed to be willing to give and take.

Within a few weeks, Sharon underwent a dramatic change. I didn't rescue Helen, because when Sharon again felt excluded, Helen knew how to handle the situation herself. Helen was happy to report that she followed the simple strategies (validating and encouraging problem-solving) and that Sharon was able to move through her emotions. Helen also reported two months later that Sharon had developed more confidence when it came to dealing with friends.

When parents contact us about such problems and we try to solve them, we're telling them much the same message as we do with our students when we try to solve their problems: that it's our responsibility to fix them, not theirs. Kids *need* to experience challenges and struggles naturally so they can learn to find solutions and be independent. All such struggles are in our children's lives so they can learn and mature. That's why struggle is good. It's a normal feature of life to be rejected socially, argue with friends, or find school hard. Yet our society thinks this is unacceptable. Helicoptering (from parents or teachers) results in more-anxious kids who lack coping and self-regulation skills. Kids don't develop anxiety from experiencing struggle, discomfort, or challenges and having a safe place to work through them. They develop anxiety from repeatedly being rescued and thus not being able to sit through and process their feelings.

ACADEMIC CONCERNS

Another experience teachers commonly encounter is parents who believe their child isn't being challenged enough or that we're not meeting parents' expectations. Obviously, parents should advocate for their children at times, but teachers nonetheless need to learn how to respond to parents while maintaining boundaries and rescuing neither parents nor children. I'm not encouraging teachers to simply ignore complaints about students not being challenged enough. We should always examine our practices and ask for help if we're unsure how to push kids more. However, anytime we receive such a complaint, we should keep our teacher authority and be open to understanding and validating parents' emotions. We should recognize that parents only want what's best for their children, but don't necessarily realize that (if it comes out through blame or reactivity) they're going about it the wrong way.

I know this situation intimately because I've been *that* parent! Remember how I used to blame others for my son's struggle? Well, I also needed to be responded to with empathy, have my feelings validated, and be given a safe space for me to feel heard. When that happened, I could work with the teacher without anger. I know all too well that some of the most difficult parents are those who need validation and non-rescuing the most!

So, our aim in this chapter is not to ignore or not support parents, but to change the conversation with them. We can become collaborative problem-solvers with parents, validate feelings, set boundaries, develop teacher authority, and move into a healthier dynamic, especially when dealing with angry moms and dads. Whether the parent's issue is related to the social or academic concerns of their child, these guidelines will help shift the conversation. ❧

STEPS TO USE WITH PARENTS

Krissy writes: 1) *Validate feelings or concerns.* As with students, when a parent is upset or concerned it's essential to move into a place of validation. When teachers do this, a receptive space is opened for teachers to listen and for parents to be heard. The space affirms the parent's viewpoint, which helps de-escalate any emotions or frustrations of the parent. Some examples of this are (you may need to keep repeating a variety of these responses):

- "That's frustrating. I imagine that it's painful for Jenny to feel rejected and for you to witness it."
- "I hear your frustration."
- "Yes, that does sound difficult."
- "Yes, I hear what you're saying."
- "Those are good points, and that makes sense."
- "I understand what you're feeling, because I'm also a parent."
- "Thank you for bringing this to my attention. This is an important issue."
- "I appreciate your letting me know about your child's struggle."

2) *Collaborate and problem-solve.* Being receptive and validating concerns help emotional upsets subside and the rational mind to come forth. It's critical not to engage in any problem-solving if the parents are still emotionally upset or reactive, since this can lead to more blaming

or wanting the teacher to fix the problem. Stay in a place of validation and listen until there's a shift toward rationality.

Once there is rationality, teachers can set the tone that we (parents and teacher) are going to collaborate to solve the problem. For example, if the child has a reading delay the teacher will create an academic plan, perhaps working with a specialist each Wednesday, and ask parents to follow through with a home plan, which might include the student reading to a parent each night. Collaboration means a shared ownership and responsibility for addressing the problem.

Many times, it will be important to make the student a part of these meetings, so the child takes ownership in problem-solving and follows through with the identified actions. The student could be in first grade and agree to read with a parent every night, or a tenth-grader who will hand in all weekly homework assignments on time. Again, students need to be involved in taking ownership of school or academic issues.

3) *Reframe struggle.* Throughout this process and throughout the school year, it's vital to keep reframing struggle as essential lessons for building social resilience in life. When problems occur during the school year, it's essential to see the *value* of the problem as a developer of skills, in addition to creating an action plan to solve it. This could even be articulated to kids: "What do you think is the value of this problem? What skill do you think you need to learn here?" Doing this immediately changes the relationship to the problem. It becomes a challenge or game to understand why the problem is occurring.

Most students today want to be considered "normal" and fear they're not normal if they have a problem. It can be hard to challenge this notion, but the internet and social media offer many examples of people failing and struggling and ultimately triumphing. Students could be assigned to write a biography of someone who turned their difficulty into success. This reframe should be consistently reinforced throughout the school year. I learned recently that soccer star and celebrity David Beckham is highly sensitive and extremely shy. I shared this observation with a sensitive and shy boy, who lacked role models since most men in mainstream culture are portrayed as tough.

4) *Engagement: Leaning in.* Whenever we have the urge to back away from a problem as teachers or parents, the best remedy is usually to lean in. If we feel an internal resistance to a parent, student, or classroom situation, it's time to lean in. Leaning in means fully engaging and opening oneself up to the problem, person, and situation. Being available to parents, checking in with them, and staying present help teachers show up. Leaning in enables us to diffuse internal resistance, which parents may feel and pick up on. I know in my work as a parent coach that when I offer a parent emergency support ("Call if you feel stuck!") and make myself more available, parents will call me less. Knowing I am one call away is reassuring to parents. I find they're more likely to problem-solve on their own and only call if it is a genuine emergency. On the other hand, with no emergency support established, I might get more frequent emails from parents, wanting help with parenting. Whenever you're annoyed, resistant, or frustrated, leaning in helps. Leaning in isn't owning the problem; it's a means of staying emotionally engaged and supportive to parents.

To conclude, collaborative problem-solving is a way to work with parents in a team approach that allows parents to remain responsible for their emotions and fears. Additionally, by staying engaged with parents throughout the year, they feel supported with their issues or challenges with their child. Being proactive helps teachers forge collaborative relationships with parents that produce good outcomes.

part 2

THE EIGHT SKILLS

chapter 8

TEACHING THE SKILLS

THE AIM OF this part of the book is to provide exercises that support the development of internal resiliency. These skills are best taught within the framework of the Four Ingredients. Students will then feel more emotionally safe and ready to engage in these exercises. Each skill will be taught and then applied to the elementary-, middle-, and high-school grades. For elementary-school grades, these skills can be taught in the context of the classroom with the homeroom teacher, with possible support from guidance as needed. For middle and high school, these skills could be taught in health and/or wellness class, and/or in an advisory group. Every school can integrate the material in the way that best suits their school environment. These exercises will take students' learning further and will allow it to become more integrated and embodied.

APPLYING THE FOUR INGREDIENTS TO THE GRADES

Through my wilderness work and parent coaching, and also as a parent myself, I've learned that all these concepts can be applied to children of all ages and in all grades. However, these concepts do not end at age eighteen. Even young adults still struggle with delayed maturation, ownership, accountability, and emotional regulation.

I work with parents of eighteen- to twenty-three-year-olds, who still blame their life disappointments and negative feelings on their parents, so this shift in ownership is a life-long process. I recently wrote an article where I told a story about my letting my then–four-year-old be sad and experience her emotions. The editor told me that he always wants to fix his nineteen-year-old daughter's feelings of sadness, so he felt the article applied to him. These concepts are universal. The shifts that Sarah made in her fourth-grade classroom are certainly transferrable to all grades, although it might take some adapting and creativity. In this chapter, we break down the application to different age groups.

ELEMENTARY: (K–4)

Obviously, younger grades are an ideal time to establish emotional-resiliency skills. K–4 is a time when young students are often brimming with emotions. Separation anxiety from leaving parents and caregivers, social anxiety in the mix of a new environment, emotional regulation issues, and frustration at being introduced to classroom learning and academics—all these are a part of a young student's experience. Emotional dysregulation or tantrums are still something students struggle with in the home environment. Kids can show up at school with a range of emotions on the surface. Yet, elementary-school students still have an openness and natural vulnerability that make them ideal for teachers to begin to instill these concepts in. The sooner young people are exposed to this material (and if possible reinforced at home), the stronger the child's coping and resiliency skills will be later on.

MIDDLE SCHOOL: (5–8)

Middle school is an awkward time. Students are more self-conscious and susceptible to peer pressure. Hormonal shifts through puberty see a corresponding drop in boys' and girls' self-esteem. A ten-year-old can feel on top of the world; two years later, that same child can be overwhelmed by self-judgment and insecurity. Additionally, middle-schoolers are more guarded emotionally, potentially suppressing emotions beneath a superficial "coolness"; cliques and the subtle bullying of exclusion among girls peak. My daughter's science teacher explained it as akin to primates establishing order and status in their groups. Middle-school boys tend to be hyperactive, impulsive, and inappropriate, egging each other on. For many boys and girls in middle school, physical maturation precedes emotional maturation, and all are operating with an underdeveloped pre-frontal cortex, where judgment and executive functioning tend to be a step behind impulsivity and reactivity.

I recently worked with a local middle school teaching emotional wellness and was surprised to hear many students speaking openly and vulnerably about their anxiety, guilt, and sadness, to name only a few emotions. They talked honestly about their inability to cope with these emotions and how they acted out of them. (It may have been my bias, but I was struck by how open the boys were; as a therapist, I'd found adolescent girls much more willing to share their feelings.) My program of emotional wellness had provided an opportunity for the middle-schoolers to name their ordinary, daily emotions, something their parents and teachers tended to overlook, side-step, or fix. If during this awkward yet critical time, when students have delicate egos and uncertain levels of confidence, we can teach internal-resiliency skills, my experience has shown me that kids will find considerable relief and support.

HIGH SCHOOL: (9–12)

Just because a student is in high school, it doesn't mean that he or she is more capable of identifying feelings, owning emotions, or accounting for behavior. In fact, the ages of fourteen to eighteen are full of avoidance, blame, escalating emotions, defiance, and lying—not to mention disorganization, executive-functioning mishaps, screen addiction, and seeking instant gratification in any form. High school is a prime time to teach ownership, accountability, self-organization, task-completion, and follow-through. Mirroring emotions is somewhat harder in the classroom, as many kids in this age group have already learned to stuff feelings as deep within themselves as possible. Many students may appear "fine"—even high-achieving, outgoing, and cheerful. But that doesn't mean there aren't internal struggles, roiling emotions, and possibly inadequate coping at home. Whereas some students may more obviously struggle with their emotions, sensitive emotional attunement on the teacher's part can help less demonstrative kids.

Children's cognition in high school has moved beyond the concrete thinking of elementary and middle school, to be much more abstract and nuanced. This means that teenagers can develop insight into their own behavior or difficulties and be more self-aware. What teens need most is to use that self-awareness to make good choices rather than be swayed by peer pressure or negative outside influences, which seem to lurk around every corner. Emphasizing the development of these skills is critical to giving teens internal resiliency to navigate the turbulent waters of high school.

SKILLS TO TEACH

The eight specific skills essential for all ages (adjusted to the three grade groupings) are:

1) Feelings Checks
2) Emotional Attunement
3) Assertive Communication
4) Ownership of Problems and Problem-Solving
5) Executive Functioning and Organizational Awareness
6) Mindfulness Practices: Sitting with Feelings and Discomfort
7) Perspective Taking
8) Delayed Gratification

chapter 9

SKILL #1—FEELINGS CHECKS

TO BEGIN THIS exercise, get a big white-board and write many different emotions with different color markers. It might look something like this:

Sad   **Worried**   *Happy*   Content

Frustrated   **Guilty**   Embarrassed

Jealous   Anxious

                    MAD   Confident

Disappointed   EXCITED

            Empathic

Calm   **UPSET**

Joyful   Scared   Betrayed   ANGRY

1) *Ask students to do a feelings check.* Ask them to take a few deep breaths, turn inward, and identify what they're feeling. Students can scan the board and see what word most resonates with their emotional state.

2) *Ask students to write the feeling word* in a journal and invite anyone to share their emotion. (I recommend this be optional and student-led. In

my experience, kids typically want to share feelings; when one or two students speak up, it creates a more welcoming atmosphere for others to do so.)

3) *Frame the question*: "Are some of these feelings good and some bad?" (Remember: we typically don't see emotions as neutral, and we label and judge them "happy = good"; "angry = bad.")

4) *Teaching moment*: "What if I told you that all the emotions on this board are neutral, neither good nor bad? Emotions simply give us information about how we feel. *Behavior* is what's good or bad, healthy or unhealthy. For example, anxiety is a normal human emotion; all of us feel anxious. However, if we're anxious and don't go to work or school, then that could be an unhealthy choice. Anger in and of itself is simply informing us that we don't like something or that we might need to set limits or tell someone *No*. Anger is only a problem if we act it out and punch a wall or yell at someone." This moment may then lead to a discussion about how we judge emotions in ourselves and in others.

5) *Ask students to scan the board* and pick out a color they're most drawn to at the moment, and write the color down.

6) *Frame the question*: Ask students: "Are some of these colors good and some bad?" Usually, this question is met with laughter, though some kids may have opinions about colors.

7) *Teaching moment*: "Colors only have the meaning we attach to them. There's no inherent label of good or bad for colors."

8) *Discussion questions*: 1) "Why do we attach labels of good and bad to feelings and not colors?" 2) "Can you imagine a world without feelings?" 3) "Can you imagine a world without colors?" Observe: "The

color spectrum makes our world rich and alive; emotions bring our world to life. Life would be pretty dull without colors or emotions."

9) *More discussion questions*: 1) "How do we feel positive about our emotions, whether we are happy or sad?" 2) "Is it possible to not judge what we feel but instead accept our feelings as information?" 3) "Is it possible to see our emotions in a neutral way, like we may view a color?"

APPLICATION TO THE GRADES

I have done this exercise with fourth, fifth, and sixth graders, college students, and even adults. It applies to all ages. Nonetheless, here are some recommended adjustments:

Angry, irritated, annoyed, frustrated, irate, and agitated — **MAD**

FEAR — Afraid, panicky, anxious, worried, restless, scared, overwhelmed, and tense

Happy, content, excited, at ease, thrilled, joyful, calm, elated, confident, hopeful, and relaxed — **GLAD**

SAD — Powerless, depressed, sorrowful, grief-struck, compassionate, and empathetic

BAD — Guilty, ashamed, embarrassed, regretful, remorseful, and betrayed

K–4: Use basic feeling words: *mad, sad, glad, bad,* and *fear.* Show pictures of faces with different basic emotions and ask students to identify them. Perhaps ask the students to draw face pictures of each feeling so there's a sense of what all the different emotions mean. Emphasize the use of colors (markers, crayons) for their journals to correlate to different feelings. Red could denote *mad*; yellow could be *happy.* Talk about how all colors are good, just like all feelings. Encourage students to identify and label their emotions through different transitions in the day, such as in the morning or after recess. This helps build resiliency skills and emotional self-awareness. Encourage a tone of acceptance for all emotions, that they provide information, and that students always have a choice how to react to them.

5–8: In this age group, you can add fifteen to twenty feeling words. Kids may be open enough to want to share feelings. It's worth setting some boundaries; for instance, that all feelings are not to be discussed outside of the group. You can recommend that students write a feeling word for each day in their journal and attach a color to each feeling. Emphasize the non-judgmental aspect of colors. Kids this age are becoming self-conscious and clique-y, so it might be worth allowing students to spread out in the classroom so they have individual space to check in with their feelings. Again, encourage a tone of acceptance for all emotions and emphasize that feelings are information. Students then always have a choice of their behavior.

9–12: Use twenty to forty feeling words, as students in high school possess a much larger vocabulary. You can add words like *chill, panicked, irritated,* even *depressed,* which will relate more to teens. Hand out feelings sheets for each student to have their own copy (such as the one in diagram 3). Depending on the emotional safety of the school or classroom, some kids may want to share, and others would rather not. Accept their boundaries. With teens, you can try to create more safety through students journaling about their emotions. Integrate a daily journal feelings check to make the practice more normal and accepted. Using colors will also depend on the group: more artistic children may be more drawn to colors than others. Again, adopt an accepting tone of what resonates most with each student.

With this older age group, many students may be more fixed in their views—such as anger and anxiety are *bad,* and happy is *good.* However, I've found high-school students surprisingly open to this material, since their inner critic and internal self-judgment of emotions are quite developed. Teens usually welcome the chance to view their anxiety, anger, and sadness in a new light.

Be open-minded in the discussion, and encourage and challenge different opinions. Have examples at the ready about how anger can produce positive outcomes (such as the Civil Rights Movement) or how anxiety is not confined to humans—such as with primates. You can note that anxiety isn't a failure or an indication something is wrong with a person, but may be a natural physical reaction, such as the fight-or-flight response when we feel threatened. Encourage students to think of real-world examples of how the only thing wrong with emotions is when we react to them and/or act them out. (You might need to emphasize that you're not referring to a medical diagnosis—such as bipolar disorder, panic disorder, clinical anxiety, or depression—but to ordinary human emotions, such as panic or unhappiness. Many kids today feel that being sad or worried means they might have depression or an anxiety disorder. This exercise aims to remove shame from the normal range of human emotions and does not involve medical conditions.)

chapter 10

SKILL #2—EMOTIONAL ATTUNEMENT

THE NEXT STEP after feelings checks and identifying emotions is to teach children how to process emotions. Unfortunately, kids aren't taught to process their feelings: most model their parents' response to their feelings in a nonverbal, unconscious process. If Mom escalates anxiety or Dad yells when he's mad, children tend to do the same. Of course, kids also enter the world with wiring that may be different from their parents, so not everything is the parents' responsibility! But transmission from parent to child tends to come via modeling.

It's a rare parent who intentionally sits down and teaches his or her children to "process their feelings." Parents may hug a child who's crying or hurt, set a limit on a child who's angry and yelling, or try to fix a child's disappointment or anxiety. But without an intentionality around such gestures, much of what is modeled are default patterns, such as telling kids how they "should" feel, getting frustrated at their emotions, or rescuing children from their feelings.

In my experience, students usually welcome the opportunity to *learn* about emotions. Many adults seem to expect kids to know what to do with their feelings (such as anxiety or anger), but kids don't know. Without the skills in place, children gravitate to dealing with uncomfortable emotions through food, sugar, video games, screens, and even drugs and alcohol. The gap between adult expectations about kids' ability to handle worry, sadness, and anger and children's lack of skills or awareness of what to do can be filled by the techniques in *Brave Parenting* and *Brave Teaching*.

I've found the metaphor of the river of emotions to be an effective way to teach about processing feelings.

River of Emotions

tired, sad

calm, present, engaged

anxious, tense

relieved, relaxed

Emotions are transient and moving
through us all day.

I talked about the river of emotions earlier. What needs to be emphasized here is that, like a river in its journey from source to ocean, emotions change. We might wake up tired, anxious, sad, or rested and content. A few hours later, we may be worried, frustrated, annoyed, sad, excited, spaced out, nervous, disappointed, relieved, restless, and so on. By the afternoon, we may be experiencing different emotions, as well as in the evening and at bedtime.

Floating on different emotional currents over the course of the day is normal and healthy—for children and adults. When emotions are transient and change, they're being processed; in fact, given that research shows that emotions last from three to thirty minutes *when we allow ourselves to feel*, we may not have time to be too reactive to an emotion. It's when emotions get blocked or stuck that stress and negative coping arise. When we don't want to feel, we're not processing our emotions. Instead, we're damming our emotional rivers.

Damming the River

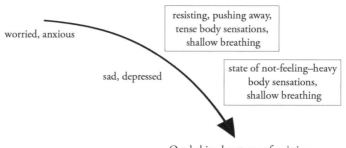

worried, anxious

resisting, pushing away,
tense body sensations,
shallow breathing

sad, depressed

state of not-feeling–heavy
body sensations,
shallow breathing

Our habitual patterns of resisting
create a constant state of stress.

Most of us unconsciously dam our emotional rivers when we experience emotions that make us uncomfortable. The dam is our internal judgment or resistance about what we feel, which, instead of just feeling the emotion, we run a story about in our heads. We ruminate, perseverate, overthink. You cannot handle an emotion by thinking it through; it must be felt and processed by the body.

Young people dam their emotions in a number of ways. Instead of feeling the emotion, they block and resist it. They think about the story, blame others, consider themselves victimized, act out their emotions, or look for rescue or escape. The dam is the place from which all addictions and negative coping emerge.

Damming Kids' Emotional Rivers

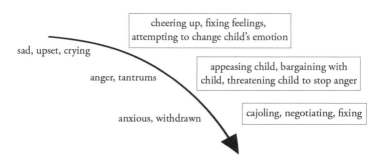

sad, upset, crying

cheering up, fixing feelings,
attempting to change child's emotion

anger, tantrums

appeasing child, bargaining with
child, threatening child to stop anger

anxious, withdrawn

cajoling, negotiating, fixing

Parents, teachers, coaches, counselors—we all unconsciously dam kids' emotions every day, when we tell them how to feel or fix their emotions and rescue them. There is no more-empowering lesson for us to teach children than the ability to be responsible for their own emotional management. It applies to the development of the whole child: emotional, social, academic.

This is how teachers can respond to emotional processing.

Refrain, Listen, and Validate Emotion

tired, sad

"That *is* sad."

anxious, worried

"It *is* scary to try new things."

frustrated

"That sounds frustrating."

Validation helps keep kids'
emotional currents moving.

VALIDATION AND SELF-VALIDATION

When we oppose or try to fix students' feelings, we act as a dam and build pressure. When we allow students to feel, we allow the river to flow and help emotions subside. Validating students allows them to feel they're heard. Furthermore, by teaching kids to self-validate, and not rely on an adult to do so, we provide them with an essential life skill.

Self-validation is the antidote to the inner critic. Self-validation is not about finding an excuse to blame others or play the victim, but is a lifelong self-care skill that allows children and students to be their own friend. The following statements are self-validating:

- "It's OK I'm sad. I just got in a fight with a friend. I'm going to let myself feel sad."

- "I can feel my anxiety. I'm going to let myself feel anxious. This is a normal response from my body before a test."
- "I feel my anger. I'm angry because in my mind I wanted things to go differently. I realize I cannot control how external events go. My feelings are important. I'm going to allow myself to feel mad, while working to accept the situation."

RIVER OF EMOTIONS EXERCISE

For this exercise, you can use the diagrams in this book or draw your own on a white-board.

1) Teach students about the emotional river and how it runs through us. Use this metaphor to show how emotions are transient and can be processed by allowing ourselves to feel our emotions.

2) Teach students about how they or other adults dam their emotional rivers and prevent themselves from processing feelings.

3) Teach students about self-validation: how it helps them get unstuck, allows them to have a positive relationship with their feelings, and keeps their emotional currents moving.

4) Teach students how they may dam a friend's river. Indicate how, although their intentions may be good, they may be telling a friend not to feel. For example, saying, "There's nothing to worry about" (when a friend may really be worried) or "Cheer up" (instead of listening and validating a friend's feeling). This is the basis of empathy.

5) *Role-play*: Ask each student to find a partner and then ask one ("the sharer") to share a feeling (which can be real or made-up) with the other ("the listener"). Have the listener first dam the river (e.g., "Don't worry about it") and then validate (e.g., "That sounds frustrating";

"I imagine that was difficult to deal with"; "That must be anxiety-provoking"). Then, switch roles and repeat. Compare and contrast one with the other.

6) *Discussion*: Debrief the exercise. Ask the students to share their thoughts on the role-play. Ask the "the sharer" if it felt better to have their feeling "fixed" or "validated." Discuss how damming and validation relate to the students and how both play out in their lives.

Note: It's important to point out that validating children's emotions does *not* mean that kids get what they want or don't have to follow a rule. Kids escalate their emotions to "get their way." This exercise's premise is based on kids feeling safe enough to feel so we don't have to rescue a student from an emotion for them to feel better. Validating a child's anxiety or fear that she or he can't complete the test doesn't mean the child gets out of sitting the exam. That's why it's essential to separate the child's emotion and thoughts and allow the child to problem-solve and be resourceful. This is where emotional resiliency comes in. So, in this scenario, the student is allowed to feel fearful, is validated, and *still* has to take the test.

GRADE APPLICATION

K–4: Younger children are kinesthetic, which means they want to learn with their whole bodies and not just their minds. When you're explaining the diagrams, you may want to have the students flow around the room, embodying their emotional river. Then, in the diagram of the dam, you might ask students to face a wall, and ask them how it feels to be blocked. Teach self-validation. Ask students how they can remove their dams, allow themselves to feel, and keep their emotional currents moving. A role-play might involve two volunteers, with one student sharing a worry or struggle and the other validating the feeling. Or the whole class can partner up. Depending on the age of the class, the teacher might have to take a firm hand in guiding the role-play. Then, the teacher should debrief the role-play.

The river and dam metaphors (in conjunction with the feelings check) form powerful tools that teachers can keep utilizing throughout the school year.

5–8 and 9–12: With these age groups, teachers can move through the diagrams of the exercise. Remember to create space for students to discuss and share, but make it optional. Some students may be dealing with difficult life situations and may require the support of a guidance counselor. This curriculum is designed for teaching students a way to process their feelings as a skill, and not for providing therapy. Nonetheless, it's possible to create space for feelings and sharing. There's no need to dig into the content of what students describe; you can simply thank them for sharing and see if it sparks others to speak up.

Middle- and high-school children welcome this period of honest emotional sharing or awareness, since many are anxious or self-conscious about their external selves (how they dress or how they're seen by peers, such as sporty or artsy), and are neglecting their inner selves. Sharing feelings can allow barriers to drop and create more safety and connection for students. You might ask them to write three to five self-validating statements in their journal, so students have an opportunity to learn and experience what this feels like.

You can allow students to partner up for the role-play. However, it's best to have teachers or assistants floating through the group to make sure students are on task and understand the assignment. There's usually an interesting discussion afterward. Some students might think it's better to be rescued or cheered up than validated, because it's what they're used to at home. Such a response is perfectly acceptable, since the aim of the exercise is to teach how to process emotions and encourage others to do the same. Rescuing, after all, can feel good. Nonetheless, as we've discussed, rescuing tends to not be as empowering in the long term.

Return to the metaphor of the emotional river throughout the year, whether you're a seventh-grade homeroom teacher or an eleventh-grade advisor. The metaphor can be a touchstone for when you see students stuck academically, socially, or emotionally. In addition to the feelings checks, students can write a self-validation in their journal daily or weekly. Most kids in middle and high school are hungry for external validation as this is an important part of ego development: *I am good at soccer. I am smart in science. I am a voracious reader.* That said, children who rely solely on external validation, are going to experience this period of life as very tumultuous. That's why learning the habit of self-validation plants the seed for more internal stability and resilience, and why self-validating statements ("It's OK to feel anxious if I don't have a friend to sit with at lunch"; "I'm a good friend"; "I like my outfit today"; "I did well in the school play") are so valuable. When we don't teach self-validation or self-affirmations, the child's inner critic is sure to jump in.

chapter 11

SKILL #3—ASSERTIVE COMMUNICATION

ASSERTIVE COMMUNICATION IS an essential skill not actively taught to students. In its absence, kids learn the communication methods modeled by the adults they're exposed to, whether parents, family members, teachers, coaches, or media outlets. The range of communication styles depends on the children's environment. When these models are integrated into schools, kids aren't just learning the default patterns they've been exposed to (which could be healthy or unhealthy); they're learning how to communicate in school as part of their education.

COMMUNICATION CONTINUUM

All communication has both verbal and nonverbal aspects. It's important to emphasize this to students, as communication is much more than what is said. The simple question, "How are you doing?" could be asked assertively, passive-aggressively, aggressively, offhandedly, indifferently, or earnestly—each of which would connote a different message: "I don't really care about you" (indifference); "I really care about you," (assertiveness); "What's wrong with you?" (passive-aggression); or "Get out of my face" (aggression). Young people in particular, since they're looking for validation, are highly sensitive to tone, facial expressions, and body language. To omit learning about nonverbal communication is to ignore an essential aspect of young peoples' everyday lives.

NONVERBAL COMMUNICATION

Nonverbal communication includes facial expression, verbal tone, and body language:

> *Facial Expression*: This includes eye contact (or lack of), smiling, frowning, and a relaxed or tense face. These give emotional information.
> *Verbal Tone*: The tone of voice gives information about the speaker's message. A speaker's tone can reveal tension, frustration, or amusement, etc. It can be hard or soft, warm or cold.
> *Body Language*: A speaker's body can be open (chest expanded, arms wide, and legs apart) or closed (arms or legs crossed protectively). It can reveal emotional clues: like wringing hands (anxiety); a red face (embarrassment); a clenched fist (anger); a face that's covered (sadness) or turned away (upset); or jumping up and down (excited).

In addition to verbal communication, which tends to be more straightforward, nonverbal communication can provide information about the emotions within the speaker's words. Emotional attunement can allow teachers to mirror to students the nonverbal communication to gauge more about what a child is feeling.

For example, the teacher might say, "I noticed you were looking at your desk [poor eye contact] most of the day. How are you feeling today?" Or "I see you bouncing around with your feet. Are you feeling restless? Would you like to go take a lap around the field [or hall]?" (This last observation is hugely beneficial for those kids who need more activity and fresh blood to their brain in order to learn!)

The continuum of both verbal and nonverbal communication can be displayed in a chart:

COMMUNICATION CONTINUUM

→ GOAL ←

WITHDRAWN	PASSIVE/AVOIDANT	ASSERTIVE	PASSIVE-AGGRESSIVE	AGGRESSIVE
(nonverbal) Ignoring Not talking Closed body language Poor eye contact Stalling Finding distractions	*(nonverbal)* Rolling eyes Hunched shoulders Closed arms Poor eye contact *(verbal)* "I think ____." Complaining Changing the subject "I don't know." "Whatever." "Fine."	*(nonverbal)* Open body language Good eye contact Relaxed shoulders *(verbal)* "I" statements: "I think ____." "I feel ____." "I hope ____." "I believe ____." "I want ____."	*(nonverbal)* Defensive or guarded body language Emotionally triggered (not calm) *(verbal)* Blame Manipulation Sarcasm "You" statements: "You made me feel ____." "I feel that you ____." "It's your fault."	*(nonverbal)* Posturing Hitting Intimidating Tense body language Loud tone *(verbal)* Yelling Threats Bullying Aggression Blame

NONVERBAL COMMUNICATION EXERCISE

1) *Role-play*: Ask students to pair up to role-play nonverbal communication. One student has to think of an emotion and, without words, use nonverbal language to communicate the emotion. The other partner has to guess the emotion. Then, switch roles.

2) *Discussion*: Ask the students to debrief the exercise within their partner group. Did each partner guess right? Did nonverbals match the emotion they were intending?

3) *Group discussion*: Debrief as a group. Ask students to share their experiences with the group.

4) *Discussion questions*: Is nonverbal communication in itself effective communication? Do we read cues incorrectly? Can we inaccurately project our beliefs onto others? For example: "Jenny didn't eat lunch with me today so she must be mad at me." Discuss.

GRADE APPLICATION

K–4: For younger grades it might be best to have two volunteers come to the front, where one is told a feeling word by the teacher and has to communicate nonverbally to a partner. Due to younger children's shorter attention spans, it might be harder to have them partner up. This age group is likely to enjoy this experiential exercise.

5–12: Run the exercise as described above.

COMMUNICATION CONTINUUM EXERCISE

1) Write the communication continuum on the board. Go over each type of communication. Discuss what assertive communication is and why it is effective communication. When communication is not assertive, it tends toward the passive or aggressive.

2) Experiential learning: with either tape or sticky notes on the floor, mark the communication continuum from withdrawn to aggressive across the room. Ask the students to form groups of two or three. Give each group a scenario on a note card. Here are some examples:

- Timmy (fifth grade) felt the boys playing kickball were being unfair, so he shoved one and walked away.
- When a new student walked over to Hazel's group (seventh grade), Hazel turned her back on her and began laughing with her friends.
- Mrs. A. asked her student Marisa (eighth grade) why she didn't hand in her homework. Marisa kept talking about how fun the water park was.
- Brian (third grade) told his mother when he got home, "It's your fault I didn't eat the lunch you packed, because it was gross."
- Stacey (ninth grade) was so mad at her grade on her math test that she slammed her hand on the desk five times.
- Jack (fifth grade) told his friend (fourth grade), "You annoy me when you constantly follow me around."
- James (tenth grade) told his mother that it was his science teacher's fault that he didn't pay attention in class: "My science teacher is so boring."
- At recess, Ari (fourth grade) told his friend that if he didn't let him be in charge of the game then he wouldn't be invited to his birthday party.
- When Becky (ninth grade) came home from school she went to her room and refused to come out for the rest of the evening.
- When Melissa (sixth grade) knew SBACs (state testing) was the next day, she felt so nervous she told her teacher, "I feel worried about testing tomorrow."

3) Ask the students to figure out which type of communication best describes the scenario on the note card. Ask one group member to stand on the spot in the communication continuum marked on the floor.

4) Ask each student in the communication continuum to read the note card, and say why they believe the card matches the communication style they're standing on. Then, ask the student to put the communication from the note card into the assertive format of I feel, I think, I believe, I hope, or I want. Ask the group if this is more effective communication.

5) *Discussion*: Come back to a circle and discuss the exercise. Ask if this exercise was relevant to the students' lives.

GRADE APPLICATION

4–12: I believe this practice can start as young as fourth grade and go through high school. To make it relevant to the different age groups, more scenarios of the different communication styles can be written for the intended grade. I've done this exercise with adults, and it's eye-opening, as so much daily communication is unconscious and habitual. This exercise increases self-awareness and helps students learn that assertive communication is the most effective.

chapter 12

SKILL #4—OWNERSHIP OF PROBLEMS AND PROBLEM-SOLVING

(*Note*: In this section, I refer to what I call "safe struggles." These include everyday difficulties around emotions, behaviors, and learning. I'm not referring to abuse or any trauma a child may face. In such situations, additional therapeutic support is recommended.)

OWNERSHIP AND PROBLEM-solving are best taught through the metaphor of the life-trail. As we've seen, the life-trail represents students' unique lives from birth onward. Each student's life-trail is littered with different rocks and boulders, cliffs and uncluttered pathways. As we've seen, the difficult terrain represents life's obstacles. We all have our own; we need to accept we have them and learn how to surmount them. If we fail to do the former, it's as if we're sitting down on the life-trail, refusing to move forward. Only if we recognize the problem confronting us will we develop the ability to solve it.

Essential to this metaphor (and life) is reframing the boulders and obstacles as opportunities. This may appear counter-intuitive, as many of life's barriers aren't inherently positive. Reframing is critical because many young people today face seemingly insurmountable hurdles, and students may feel stuck or unmotivated, or distract themselves from the boulder blocking their way forward. Yet, teachers still need to help students learn; there must be a framework to create forward movement.

As I argued earlier in the book, learning how to scale or find a way around obstacles is crucial for developing resiliency, maturity, and skills for the challenge awaiting us around each corner in our life-path. Obstacles also provide an opportunity to grow, learn, and discover new abilities. For instance, not making the soccer team in high school might turn a teen toward the school play, which could launch an acting career. And, finally, unless those rocks and boulders are acknowledged and dealt with by the child, the latter will not learn and grow. There's no shortcut: we can only mature and become skilled when we face our life's obstacles.

LIFE-TRAIL EXERCISE: PART ONE

1) Draw a diagram of the life-trail metaphor on the board.

2) Explain the metaphor and the different sections: boulders; life obstacles or problems (learning issues, behavioral or social struggles); sharp rocks or difficult emotions (emotional regulation struggles); cliffs or life-changing situations (a move, a family change, a school change, an illness) (Note: the bigger the obstacle, the greater the growth opportunity); a smooth trail or easy going.

3) Discuss the metaphor. Of course, we all want our lives to be easy, yet is this how life really is? Do we grow and mature when life is smooth? Do rocks and boulders bring learning? Does a lesson learned in fourth grade help when we arrive in sixth grade? Will students' seeing their life-trail as continuous assist them when they face challenges? For example, a present challenge may actually prepare the child for the future.

4) Ask students to write in their journal about five life boulders, rocks, or cliffs they've faced. Ask them to describe in their journal how they

worked around or scaled these challenges, and if they did so successfully. Ask students to identify what lessons they learned as a result of these life obstacles. (This could be a classroom or homework assignment.)

5) Give the opportunity for students to share in a group discussion any examples of learning from a rock or boulder. Again, sharing needs to be optional and student-driven. However, if students are proud of surmounting a boulder and learning a lesson, it can be positive for them to share with the group and help pass on the lesson. Ask students if they can reframe future or upcoming obstacles or challenges as opportunities. Would this alter their experience of the obstacle?

GRADE APPLICATION

5–12: This exercise is best suited for students in this age range. A school could introduce the idea of the life-trail and life obstacles in fifth grade and keep building on the concepts through middle school and into high school. Emphasizing the ability to reframe challenges as opportunities and building resiliency skills are most effective when they're reinforced each year. This material is also relevant to adults.

PROBLEM-SOLVING

After teaching the lesson of the life-trail, teachers can really home in on problem-solving skills. Most adults have learned to problem-solve in their lives and careers when there was no other option. When parents over-manage and problem-solve for their kids, I frequently ask parents how they learned to problem-solve in their own lives. They often tell me they learned because it was either "sink or swim." Is there an option other than solving and fixing for students or the sink-or-swim method? How can we be more thoughtful about teaching problem-solving in life, and not just in math class? Can it be intentionally taught?

LIFE-TRAIL EXERCISE: PART TWO

1) Complete part one of the life-trail exercise.

2) Ask the students to look through their journal assignment where they had to identify how they negotiated the five obstacles on their path. If they felt they successfully surmounted the boulder, what problem-solving skill did they use?

3) With a white-board and markers, ask students to brainstorm and share problem-solving techniques and skills that helped them on their life-trail. We can also call this "Healthy Coping." Draw a line down the middle of the white-board, and on one side write down HEALTHY PROBLEM-SOLVING or UNHEALTHY COPING.

4) The flip side of healthy problem-solving is making unhealthy choices. Most students are familiar with one or two examples of negative coping or solving. Ask students to share these examples. (Make clear that in the sharing they don't have to discuss the particular struggle they faced, only the problem-solving skills or lack thereof.) The board might look something like this:

HEALTHY PROBLEM-SOLVING	UNHEALTHY COPING
Accepting the situation	Fighting the situation
Learning to accept my feelings	Blaming others
Recognizing that the way people treat me is about them not about me	Holding resentments
	Lying
Not taking things personally	Feeling like a victim
Learning more about how the world works	Having a meltdown
Telling people how I feel	Looking for someone to rescue me
Allowing myself to be sad	
Learning to take the high road	Giving up

Understanding that kindness works	Indulging in negative self-talk
Getting more organized	All addictions: food, substances, gaming, social media, and so on
Writing in my journal	
Doing things that make me happy	
Understanding it's OK to be uncomfortable	
Looking at my role in the situation	
Not reacting, but getting calm first	
Working harder	
Challenging myself	
Listening to what others feel	
Learning to take deep breaths when mad	
Engaging in positive self-talk	
Exercising	
Having hobbies	
Making friends	

Be open to the ideas the students bring forth. What I love about this exercise is that students really possess their own inner wisdom. They have the answers to their own problems, and tapping into them can be really empowering.

5) Ask students to write down a list of the healthy problem-solving skills they identify with and want to use more. Maybe keep a list posted on the classroom wall as a reminder.

6) Finally, ask students what feels better: using the healthy solutions or the negative coping? This usually starts an interesting discussion. Unhealthy choices usually feel good for about five minutes but weigh on a student's conscience, whereas healthy choices feel good over time and actually build esteem and self-worth.

GRADE APPLICATION

K–4: This age group may struggle with the more advanced concepts here, but that doesn't mean you can't teach problem-solving. What's most important to this age group when issues or conflicts arise is to ask students: "How do you want to solve this?" or "You have really good problem-solving skills. What do you think is the best way to solve this?" Validating kids helps get the wheels turning in their brain: "I think you are capable of doing that. I'm going to let you be in charge of figuring it out." These are all messages of empowerment: "It's OK if you don't know how to solve it right now. Why don't you think about it for a day, and we can talk about it more tomorrow?" Sometimes, planting a question in our minds allows our unconscious to work at it. For instance, Einstein said he often solved problems in the shower or on a walk. We want to encourage this habit in young people.

For this younger age group, what's most important is to frame obstacles and opportunities so there doesn't always have to be a negative connotation. All these responses build up the problem-solving muscles in our students and develop their capacity to move forward on their life-trails.

5–12: Running the exercise as described above will fit all these grades. The teaching of the exercise will be similar, but the differences will be in their answers. For example, healthy problem-solving and the negative-coping brainstorm session will differ between eleven-year-olds and seventeen-year-olds. The former will understand the boulders metaphor in a more concrete way and have simpler examples from life, whereas a seventeen-year-old will have a more nuanced and sophisticated understanding of the metaphor and more life experiences, and thus more and bigger boulders. Nonetheless, the exercise can be taught in a similar, straightforward way.

As with the younger age group, continue to ask fifth to twelfth graders to use their problem-solving skills to address issues, challenges, and struggles that arise in the classroom or school. Frame this in a way that empowers: you see the students as capable, creative, and resourceful. Build a classroom culture of ownership, problem-solving, and viewing obstacles as opportunities.

chapter 13

SKILL #5—EXECUTIVE FUNCTIONING AND ORGANIZATIONAL AWARENESS

WHAT BECAME CLEAR in wilderness therapy is that when nobody assumed responsibility for a student, a student assumed responsibility for him- or herself. I'd watch kids who'd recently entered the program act helpless for days on end, waiting for someone to rescue them. They'd also do their best to power struggle (through blaming or acting even more helpless) with any adult who came into view. Yet no one rescued the student.

Wilderness therapy assumes all kids have agency or freewill and can choose to give up or apply themselves. The staff aren't going to engage in any power struggles; instead, they let the students make the choice that best suits them. The wilderness is a learning container that allows kids to feel; it holds behavioral boundaries, lets kids struggle, and is physically and emotionally safe. With these four ingredients, the magic begins to happen. This is true even with those students who have ADD or executive-functioning delays, since part of students' taking ownership of their issues is for them to get to know their brains and how best to complete tasks or follow through. From my experience, ninety-nine percent of the kids choose to engage and genuinely seem happy with the choice.

As with many skills detailed in this book, organization can and needs to be taught. We teach kids everything else—how to read, tie their shoelaces, sweep the floor, do math, brush their teeth, and so on. One could argue that learning our own organizational style is one of the most essential skills for future achievements: completing high school, graduating from college, being successful in a job, managing adult life. Yet this skill is not explicitly taught. Many parents keep their kids on busy schedules—such as school, sports, music lessons, play dates—but do all the "life management" (meal planning, driving, appointment making, cleaning the house, and tidying belongings). This way kids don't have to think about organizing their lives; they just go from A to B.

An effective way to teach organization is to ask students to undertake a task—such as organizing a desk or writing a book report—and then have them study how they completed it. You can call this the "metaprocess": a process used to describe or define another. In addition to the tasks we all do every day, there is a metaprocess of how one completes the task. For example, in my household everyone empties the dishwasher a little differently: this is based on each family member's organizational skills.

Discovering the metaprocess requires a different set of analytic skills. Although I'm more "type A" and a naturally organized person, I have to admit that I don't like to analyze how I do things. I'd rather skip that and do the task itself. The truth is, however, the more I'm aware of how I organize my thoughts and complete my tasks the more self-aware I am. I've learned that I tend to organize about eighty percent of life and leave the rest to chaos and improvisation. So, I could stand to review at times whether that metaprocess is working for me!

Any learning can have process and metaprocess. Here are some examples.

K–4 EXERCISE

1) Ask students to keep their desk clean for one week. Their desks will be checked at the end of each day.

2) At the end of the week, ask the students to describe, verbally or in a written assignment, which system or organizational process they used to complete this daily task. They may have to think about it!

3) Ask students to apply this task to their backpacks for one week (checked each morning).

4) At the end of the week, ask the students to describe, verbally or in a written assignment, which system or organizational process they used to complete this daily task.

This exercise might be more basic for K–2 than for 3–4, but it can still get students' minds thinking about their metaprocess. One student may keep her desk clean at all times; another may stuff his papers in his desk and only organize it five minutes before it's checked; still others may have different systems. The point is not to see one system as better than any other, but for each student to understand how his or her own brain works. If a student isn't completing a task, add a day to the assignment so the student understands he or she is accountable for a week.

When students begin to better understand how they think through steps, they'll have more self-awareness and greater ability to know how they best organize tasks. You may ask the students to review their process and see if it worked effectively or if they'd like to make changes to their process. When you do the backpack assignment, ask students what changes were implemented between the first and second exercises.

STYLES OF ORGANIZATION AND ANXIETY

Students have different kinds of organization and anxiety. For instance, with organizational style, there is linear, circular, and visual:

1) *Linear*: These students typically create an outline and move through an assignment in a straightforward manner: beginning, middle, end, review, and complete.

2) *Circular*: These students may start in the beginning, skip to the end, return to the middle, and then start over. There is a circular and flowing way of thinking through a process.

3) *Visual*: Instead of creating an outline, these students will benefit most from drawing pictures and sequences, which help them map out the steps to take to plan their project.

With anxiety, students often have three styles:

1) *Motivator*: Some students go from anxiety to action. They make lists and outlines, and begin the project the day it is assigned. They may even finish early and hand the project in before it's due.

2) *Steady engagement*: Some students' anxiety helps bring a steady focus to an assignment. They may chip away at it each day, making progress throughout the project period to have the paper ready on time.

3) *Procrastinator*: Some students go from anxiety to avoidance. They might delay starting and perseverate on the project, meaning they think about it but don't act. These students lack internal drive and motivation and instead need the external limit of the date the assignment is due. It's likely they'll cram the assignment and complete it at the last minute. They may even turn it in late or not at all.

5–8 EXERCISE

1) Here is an exercise that could be applied in a science class. Students are asked to build a bridge out of Popsicle sticks. The bridge has to support up to fifty pounds. The assignment is due in two weeks. Alongside this, students are asked to keep notes on their metaprocess. They are asked to record every step taken or not taken if it relates to the assignment. This includes making a plan in their heads, looking up bridge models on Google, worrying for a week, finding every excuse not to begin, buying glue and Popsicle sticks at the hardware store, and the actual building and perhaps rebuilding of the model.

2) When the assignment is due, test each bridge to see if it can hold fifty pounds.

3) Ask students to write a paper about their metaprocess, their thinking, and the steps they took to complete the bridge. Then, ask the students to critique their own metaprocess. Did they go about their bridge in an effective, efficient way? Did they reach the outcome they wanted? If they were to undertake the assignment again, would they choose to do it differently?

4) Ask students to identify their organizational style and anxiety style. Does this work for them, or do they want to try to do it differently next time?

9–12 EXERCISE

1) In history class, ask students to complete a ten-page research project on a subject that relates to their classroom content. Alongside this, students are asked to keep notes on their metaprocess: to record every step taken or not taken if it relates to the assignment. This could include going to the store to buy cards on which to write notes during their

research, creating a timeline of events during this period in Google docs, making an outline first before starting any research, conducting the research, writing the paper, editing it, and so on.

2) After the assignment is completed and handed in, ask students to write a paper about their metaprocess, their thinking, and the steps they took to complete the research paper. Then, ask the students to critique their own process. Did they go about their paper in an effective, efficient way? Did they reach the outcome they wanted? If they were to do the assignment again, would they choose to do it differently?

3) Ask students to identify their organizational style and anxiety style. Do these styles work for them, or do they want to try to do them differently next time?

These assignments can be applied to any school task or lesson, so feel free to apply the metaprocess inquiry to any assignment.

chapter 14

SKILL #6—MINDFULNESS PRACTICES

Sitting with Feelings and Discomfort

MINDFULNESS PRACTICES AND meditation are increasingly coming into schools to help students with focus, attention, and emotional regulation, and to bring awareness to students' emotional and mental health. This is a positive trend and one that I believe will continue. Meditation, relaxation, and mindfulness skills give kids the tools to begin to take ownership of their inner world. They provide students with the opportunity to tune in internally, and to give attention to and care-take their thoughts, emotions, and impulses.

The Four Ingredients emphasize creating a supportive classroom environment that not only allows but encourages students to sit with discomfort. This is in direct opposition to the message most students receive at home or in society at large, where children's discomfort is fixed. Influenced by wilderness therapy, I advocate that teachers validate, allow, support, and encourage kids to sit with their feelings. This can be an underlying framework to your classroom, and not just a twenty-minute exercise during a mindfulness segment.

Discomfort, disappointment, frustration, anxiety, worry, and being overwhelmed: these are all safe to feel. What I want to emphasize is that how students learn to be with their emotions is largely a result of how emotions are modeled to the student and how adults respond to a student in distress. If a student in distress is met with a tense adult, this tends to amplify the distress; if a student in distress is met by a rescuing adult, the distress may be amplified (because it creates a dependency or feeling of powerlessness), or the rescue may help a student calm down (because the student feels supported). Neither case builds skills. If a student experiencing distress is met with a calm adult who normalizes the feeling and encourages the student to feel the emotion, then the student will move through the emotion and build skills around processing feelings.

HOW TO ENCOURAGE STUDENTS TO SIT WITH DISCOMFORT

1) *Reframing*: Encouraging and allowing struggle and discomfort in students starts with the teacher being comfortable with struggle and discomfort in the classroom. This means the teacher needs to absorb the lessons I describe in the book: all the bumps in the road are opportunities; experiencing discomfort when learning new information or being in different social situations is normal. Part of reframing discomfort is normalizing discomfort associated with being in school. For example, many students think something is wrong with them if they don't understand algebra the first time, don't have a friend to sit with at lunch, or don't like their Spanish teacher. These are normal, everyday feelings. Normalizing is a helpful way to accept and allow discomfort.

2) *Finding your own calm*: Teachers are already drawing deeply each day from the well of calmness to deal with all the variables in a classroom. They also tend to be empathic already—meaning they're sensitive and tuned into others' emotions, which is part of their desire and ability to work with children. However, working with a distressed child can wear on any adult. That's why it's important for teachers to have their own grounding techniques and mindfulness practices to

stay with a student's distress and to encourage him or her to feel. It should be emphasized that teachers are still responding to students' distress whether they're rescuing or not.

3) *View it as an experiment*: If you want to make the shift toward allowing emotions in the classroom and are worried about the outcome, you might view it as an experiment. So, for example, set a goal: For the next week, any time that a child has an upset, emotional reaction or expresses discomfort, tell yourself the following: *I will listen and allow instead of doing any action. I'll encourage the student to sit with the feeling and let him or her know the emotion is safe to feel.* Then, collect data during the week about how you responded to each episode of creating space. How did the student respond? At the end of the week, can you determine if this response had a better, worse, or same outcome? Did the shift help promote skills, such as ownership and self-regulation? Did it enable students to move through discomfort and then come back to the situation at hand? Try for yourself and note the results.

4) *Stay consistent*: As Sarah Love discovered in her school and classroom, by validating feelings, holding space, and allowing kids to feel, she created a new norm for her students. At first, it was scary because she felt she was letting go of control, because fixing is a form of control. Over time, with consistency, this new teacher–student script became Sarah's default. Every conflict, frustration, and emotional upset has become an opportunity for student ownership and skill-building. Sarah herself has become more resilient by trusting the process and seeing the positive outcomes. As she stated at the beginning of this book, in her previous years as a teacher she'd created a dependency with her students; as such, she was always anxious her students would fall apart when she wasn't around. By promoting independent skill-development in her students, Sarah no longer carries that same worry. This consistent response has created new outcomes.

MINDFULNESS SKILLS

In addition to responding to emotional distress, mindfulness skills help build students' resiliency and self-regulation. Ideally, mindfulness exercises are conducted once a week, whether in a homeroom classroom in elementary or in an advisory group in middle or high school. Whether the practice is five or thirty minutes in duration, as with all things, repetition helps.

In a society so externally focused, shifting inward is essential and for many students is a welcome relief. At school, students receive a lot of external stimulation. They look at other kids all day long and form judgments about others or themselves. Examining this inner dialogue is a useful way to gain self-awareness and introduce calmness to this internal landscape. Different techniques can draw students' attention to their senses; this process has an amazing ability to quiet the mind and bring students into the present moment. Here are some exercises to try.

K–4 EXERCISE

1) Ask students to cup their hands and hold them about six inches from their mouths. Ask students to take a big breath in and slowly exhale with pursed lips, as if they're filling with air the bowl made by their cupped hands. When the bowl is filled with air, exhale the rest. Repeat five times.

2) This quick exercise emphasizes the exhalation, which helps the body relax.

ALL GRADES EXERCISES

The following mindfulness exercises (in sound, smell, touch, and movement) draw attention through the senses to the present moment, and are excellent for students of all ages.

1) *Sound*: Use a bell, meditation chime, gong, or any other instrument that resonates. Ask students to sit cross-legged or straight back in a chair or at a desk. Ask students to listen to the sound of their own breath for one minute. Then, strike the bell or chime and ask students to place their attention from the beginning until the sound completely dissipates. Repeat three times. Leave students to settle into three to ten more minutes (depending on age) of following the sound of their own breath. Bring attention back to the group and discuss or end.

2) *Far and near sounds*: Ask students to sit cross-legged or straight back in a chair or at a desk. Ask them to listen to the sound of their own breath for one minute. Then, ask students to turn their attention to faraway sounds. What is the furthest they can hear? It could be a highway, a river, a dog barking. Allow three to five minutes for this. Then, ask students to switch their awareness to close-up sounds: their own breathing, a neighbor, or sounds in the room they're sitting in. Stay with this for three to five minutes. Then, ask students to let go of all sound. Bring attention back to the group and discuss or end.

3) *Smell—essential oils*: Pass around an essential oil for students to smell directly, or place a drop on their wrist or clothing. (Ask first about allergies.) Something uplifting is ideal: citrus, lemon, grapefruit, rosemary, peppermint, cedar, or eucalyptus. Ask students to sit cross-legged or straight back in a chair or at a desk. Ask them to listen to the sound of their own breath for one minute. Then, ask students to bring their full attention to the essential oil or any other noticeable smells. Bring attention back to the group to discuss or end.

4) *Touch—physical sensations*: Ask students to sit cross-legged or straight back in a chair or at a desk. Ask them to listen to the sound of their own breath for one minute. Now ask them to bring their attention to all physical sensations. It could be the feeling of the bottom of the chair or the cushion; their legs crossed or their hands resting on their thighs.

Then, ask students to bring awareness to internal sensations, such as air filling up their lungs, their lungs expanding, and then the feeling of air leaving their lungs. Ask students to keep their awareness on their lungs expanding for three to five more minutes. Bring attention back to the group to discuss or end.

5) *Body scan*: Ask students to lie on their backs on the floor on a mat or rug. Ask them to bring their attention to their lungs expanding and contracting as air moves in and out of their bodies. Now take students through a body scan, starting with their feet. Ask students to bring their attention to their feet, ankles, calves, and knees. Slowly move through the body parts, bringing awareness to the thighs, hips, lower back, spine, stomach, chest, and collarbone. Then the hands, wrists, forearms, elbows, upper arms, shoulders, neck, skull, face, ears, nose, eyes, and finally the top of head. Usually, this is quite relaxing. Ask students to bring their attention back to their breath, and then sit up and end.

6) *Walking meditation*: After a short sitting meditation of following their breaths for three to five minutes, ask students to spread themselves evenly in a big circle in the classroom. Ask students to slowly walk around in a circle, where all their attention is placed on the physical sensation of the foot pressing into the ground and then releasing. Then attention is placed on the next foot applying pressure to the floor. After students have made a few laps of the classroom (slowly), ask them to come back to sitting in a circle and discuss.

CONCLUSION

With each of these exercises, depending on time allotted, it may be helpful to discuss and debrief with the students. Do students feel more focused, relaxed, mindful, and/or present? How does this new awareness differ from the normal state? Ask students to note which exercises they thought might be helpful when experiencing struggle or discomfort. These techniques give an opportunity to emphasize the student's inner self, which is just as important as his or her external or outward self. Of course, ninety-nine percent of a student's attention tends to be placed on the external self, so doing these exercises and raising awareness of the interior self are essential in helping students achieve a healthy balance between inner and outer.

chapter 15

SKILL #7—PERSPECTIVE TAKING

RECOGNIZING PERSPECTIVE IS an essential skill for today's world, especially with more and more media outlets catering to narrower and narrower audiences. In the classroom, understanding different perspectives naturally occurs when studying history, social studies, or current events. When students are asked to argue one side of an issue either orally in class or in an opinion paper, they're being given an opportunity to apply perspective taking to their learning. Younger students may read books that reveal different perspectives and learn there are different sides to a story. In addition to the more academic avenue for learning about perspective taking, opportunities exist to apply it to classroom issues. Teachers can also do role-plays or experiential exercises to teach perspective taking as a life skill, not as an abstract or academic concept.

When perspective taking is taught as a skill, it can be applied to life situations actively. For example, at the start of the school year a new student, Finley, joined the eighth grade of a local public school. She'd previously attended private school. Although Finley was new to the school, her childhood best friend, Bea, was in the class. Swiftly, Bea and Finley became inseparable, which was a challenge for Bea's old best friend, Annie, who'd spent most of seventh grade hanging out with Bea. Annie felt left out and excluded. When the new dynamics became obvious to the girls' teacher and guidance counselor, the latter invited the girls to her office for some perspective taking.

Each girl was asked to share her perspective. Annie, who seemed the most upset, said: "Since Finley came to school here, I have lost Bea as a friend, and I also feel excluded by Bea and Finley." Bea responded: "I'm sorry you feel that way. My perspective is that it is hard for me to know what to do when my childhood friend Finley is now in my class. She is new and doesn't have friends, and I really want to help her adjust. You're still my friend, Annie, and you are welcome to be with me and Finley." Finley then said: "I'm sorry if I caused disruptions. It has been so great to have you in my class, Bea, and I am glad to know you as well, Annie."

The counselor then asked each student to switch seats to try to take on the perspective of the person who had been sitting in the seat. Annie took Bea's seat, Bea took Finley's, and Finley took Annie's. Each was asked to imagine herself in the new role and to see if they noticed any different feelings. Finley instantly felt empathy for Annie: "I can see it's hard when your closest school friend has a new best friend. I'm glad I can see what this feels like for you." Annie saw Bea's dilemma: "I can see you're split between me and your childhood friend, who is new. It makes sense you want to spend time with her." Then Bea, who already felt empathy for Finley's position, said: "I imagine it must feel a little bad to want attention from me but know I have other friends. I knew it was hard for you to be at a new school, but now I see that it's hard socially."

The teacher then asked the students to switch again, so each saw each student's perspective. The goal in this assignment wasn't to solve anything: no one was right and no one was wrong. The goal was to build new awareness, which could and did impact their social relationships. When the girls left the office, they already felt more bonded and closer as a result of the exercise, which helped shed some barriers and enhanced their understanding of their different roles.

Perspective taking has some key components:

1) There's no blame and no "right" or "wrong."
2) There's no need to be defensive when there's no blame.
3) There's no need for students to "build a case."
4) Students can really lean in and listen and hear others' perspectives.
5) As a result, empathy tends to naturally come forth.
6) A broader perspective helps build connection and dissolve barriers to communication.

EXERCISES FOR PERSPECTIVE TAKING: CAR ACCIDENT (GRADES 4+)

1) Split the class into groups of four or five and ask them to imagine they are a family in a car. Every group can decide who sits where and assign each member a family role (mother, father, teen, aunt, baby, child, young adult). The group decides who's driving (maybe the father, mother, aunt, or a teen). They create a scenario for a car accident.

2) Each member of the family has to write out their perspective of the accident and how it impacted them. When they are done writing their perspectives, groups can sit in a small circle, and each person reads their perspective of the accident.

3) Group discussion: Did the family members have different perspectives? Could this be based on their age, family role, or where they sat in the car?

4) When mini-groups finish up, ask a member of each group to report to the class what their group learned. What did each group discover?

5) Lead the discussion to bigger issues on how this exercise might apply to other current events or larger societal issues. Did this exercise help contribute to greater empathy or awareness of others' perspectives?

6) The discussion could even turn into current debates such as loggers (wanting jobs) versus environmentalists (wanting to save trees), or other debates where there is an opportunity to take perspectives.

Perspective taking can be used actively in the classroom when there is an issue or conflict. Asking students to hear another's perspective and/or asking students to temporarily trade places so they can imagine what it might be like to look at the conflict through an other's perspective is an excellent way to apply a life skill to real classroom issues and build it into academic learning and empathy.

chapter 16

SKILL #8—DELAYED GRATIFICATION

CHILDREN ARE GROWING up in a society of instant gratification. Smartphones have radically changed our lives; information is now shared instantly, and children have immediate distractions and rewards in the palm of their hands—whether it's a video game, social media, texting, watching a show, or a multitude of other sources of entertainment. Research shows that this instantaneous gratification has impacted our ability to focus our attention: whereas the average attention span was sixteen seconds a decade ago, it's now only eight. With these societal shifts, delayed gratification is not an ability readily seen in young people today.

Living in the wilderness is the direct opposite of our current trends. There, accomplishing anything takes a long time. If you want to move to a new site, you have to pack up camp and walk. If you want a hot dinner, you have to collect firewood, make a fire, boil water, and cook a meal. If you need more water, you have to haul it from the "front country," or fill up at a local stream. Everything is a slow and deliberate process of delayed gratification. Nonetheless, it's important to note that the effort makes the reward much more fulfilling to savor. Sitting around a campfire at night after hiking, setting up camp, and cooking a meal is incredibly relaxing and allows one to soak in the whole day. The gratification is earned and worth it and kids become accustomed to the multistep process of accomplishing tasks in the wilderness. Doing things calmly and deliberately is soothing. It builds patience, resilience, and perseverance.

When students return to their schools, homes, and communities, they return to a world of quick fixes, ultra-convenience, and instantaneity. This can be thrilling but also over-stimulating and anxiety-provoking.

BRINGING DELAYED GRATIFICATION INTO THE CLASSROOM

Like most concepts in Brave Teaching, delayed gratification can be introduced to the classroom and reinforced throughout the year as an important aspect of any goal. Setting a goal such as learning an instrument, putting on a school play, writing a book report, or doing a science project most likely involves delayed gratification. When students are accustomed to instant gratification, they may be more likely to give up on an idea if the reward or outcome seems too far away. Students may feel investing in projects is not worth the work or effort.

The 1970s Stanford marshmallow experiment has become a hallmark for indicating a child's ability to experience delayed gratification. In the study, a child was offered a marshmallow on a plate and told that he or she could eat it immediately or wait approximately fifteen minutes and receive two marshmallows. In follow-up studies, researchers found that children who were able to wait longer for the reward tended to have better life outcomes, as indicated by SAT scores, educational attainment, body mass index (BMI), and other life measures.

K–3 EXERCISE

1) Read the marshmallow experiment to your classroom (there are also some videos on YouTube).

2) Discuss the experiment and its outcome and ask students how they imagine they would fare.

3) Create a classroom experiment to test the class's ability to delay gratification. You can come up with all sorts of things.

4) Highlight and reinforce any time you see delayed gratification playing out in the class in general or specifically with students.

5) Institute an end-of-day reward, or a jar that kids can add marbles to for performing tasks and helping each other. There's a reward when it is filled.

6) Play out exercises, such as taking an immediate recess or getting a marble.

7) Encourage students to write out goals and see how delayed gratification might help them achieve them.

CONCLUSION

🌿 **SARAH WRITES:** As I reflect upon my year, I'm encouraged at the change I see in my students' ability to take responsibility for themselves and move through challenging experiences. I've watched students mature in ways I don't typically see in society. It's overwhelming to me as a professional always to be putting out fires, and it's time we taught students to accept responsibilities and learn how to solve their own problems. It's long overdue that we allow students to feel and regulate their emotions, so they're not victims of their situations but creators instead. It would be a critical shift to teach such life skills, since a fundamental goal of education is to set the road for student and life success. Students need these internal-resiliency skills.

I encourage you, as educators, to make the change. The most important thing I learned this year was how important it is to teach these skills in the first six weeks and to reinforce the concepts through the whole school year. I noticed that the more I was consistent with my response, the easier it was not to get hooked into rescuing and power struggles. The students started coming to me less and less and began solving their own problems more. The Four Essential Ingredients don't bring instant change; they must be used with consistency. As a teacher, I had to set the goal to stay the course.

I should be honest and note that I did become inconsistent at one point in the year. I was burned out and exhausted, and forgot to validate. As any teacher knows, all school years have ups and downs. Things began to slip, and I saw more students come to me, wanting me to fix a problem, situation, or an emotion for them. Realizing I was being inconsistent, I quickly reminded myself it was necessary to respond the same way in every situation. At this point, I saw how my students craved ownership and self-regulation. However, we're all capable of falling back into old patterns—whether students or teachers—and that lapse impacted the dynamics of the classroom. Fortunately, I was able to get back on track because I knew how to reset the tone, reacquire my teacher authority, and return to the basics.

As a quick before and after, let me conclude with a story of a student I'll call Alice, who was highly impacted by the ingredients in my classroom. Alice was a part of a BD (behavior disorder) classroom. At the beginning of the year, Alice couldn't own anything and would perseverate with things she couldn't control. Partner work was almost nonexistent, and she didn't have any good friendships. A daily TA "managed" her. When I first started using my Brave Teaching response, Alice struggled tremendously. Regardless of my validating her emotions, she became fixated, and it was hard for her to move out of that space and into acceptance. Alice was conditioned after many years of outbursts to respond with obsessive and repetitive statements about how she wasn't wrong and whatever it was was someone else's fault.

Recognizing the importance of a consistent response, I decided to get all the teachers (including specials, programs teachers, and TAs) on board with the same approach in every encounter with Alice. We saw an amazing turnaround in Alice's ability to self-regulate. Every teacher validated Alice's feelings; reframed struggle as normal, good, or OK; and encouraged Alice to problem-solve. Though there were challenging moments initially, by the end of the year Alice was in the general education classroom ninety-five percent of the time. Alice can now manage disagreements with integrity and takes complete responsibility for her actions, positive or negative. In the second part of the year, she had no outbursts, but instead advocated for herself when she needed a break. The change is profound, and as a result of this success, she has more esteem and has developed more friendships.

All students can achieve the ability to self-regulate, and all students need help with this skill, whether they are BD or not. Some may take longer than others because of their experiences, but all have the innate ability to problem-solve and manage their own lives, and to feel more competent and capable.

The change overall in my classroom is more than evident, and it's grown beyond my classroom into my larger school community, with many teachers and my principal taking note and wanting to embrace the approach across the school. There's less student bullying, almost no tattling, and growth and resiliency when dealing with failure. Students offer no excuses; they recognize their part in the problem; they accept compliments from others; they are able to deal with challenges (math, social rejection, group dynamics); there are fewer accusatory parental emails; there is less need to increase homework; and fewer arguments are breaking out with and between classmates. There has been an extraordinary shift in my classroom climate.

Many of you will worry about the responses you'll receive from parents when you use this philosophy in your classrooms. The truth is, you'll get some frustrated parents. Remember: the parents are also going through a shift in thinking. They're used to the teacher rescuing and fixing everything. Once you remove either, most parents will be initially uncomfortable and even frightened. Eventually, however, most parents see the change in their child's ability to self-regulate and begin to let go of control. Most parents will start to trust the process, and be willing to make changes themselves.

There are no limits to this kind of thinking. If all teachers learned how to support students and stepped back from rescuing them, we would see a tremendous change in the community as well as a decrease in anxiety and frustration. Staff and parents would be more confident and less likely to respond emotionally, thus keeping a safe environment in which students could fail and develop growth mindsets. As in every school, some teachers are positive and some negative, but many teachers—once they see how well this philosophy impacts students as well as the new outcomes—cannot help but want to learn more about it.

One of Krissy's ideas that made a huge impact on me as I followed through with Brave Teaching was that our children have their own lives, and what they do with them is not our business; what is is giving them tools and accountability. I feel the same way: as a parent and a teacher. It's not our job to manage, control, or make our students obey, but rather to help them be responsible for their own lives.

I feel a sense of accomplishment this year. Becoming a brave teacher and changing the students' experience at school has been more than gratifying; it's been life-changing for me and my practice. I will continue to refine and reflect on how I respond to students for the next school year. Brave Teaching isn't something one teacher can master quickly; it takes time, patience, and a desire for change. I'm hopeful other teachers will dive into Brave Teaching. Good luck on your journey. 🌿

KRISSY WRITES: This is a pivotal moment in American schools. There's a growing need for broader knowledge about teaching emotional resiliency, yet many school districts feel it falls outside of the curriculum. As the need among students grows, schools must respond to meet it. Since beginning this project, I've received countless requests from teachers, parents, parents on school boards, principals, parents' support-group leaders, and many others, asking me for help. Indeed, Sarah and I really couldn't write this book fast enough, because parents, teachers, and administrators need these tools and skills now. Schools cannot continue to operate in compartmentalized ways anymore, where academic knowledge comes from the classroom, physical health from the sports team, and emotional growth from a therapist. Schools need to raise whole kids and address all their needs: academic, social, emotional, physical, and so on.

This book offers teachers the tools to foster internal resiliency in their students, to reframe conflict and struggle in the classroom, and let both be part of their learning. Many teachers may feel overwhelmed about integrating this new material into their teaching. There tends to be natural resistance to change, whether from teachers or parents I work with. What I suggest is that you try it five percent of the time. Even if parents respond differently to their child—for example, validating a feeling instead of fixing it—only five percent of the time, it's an opportunity to see if it produces a different outcome. I also challenge teachers with the five-percent rule. For some, it may be a slow and gradual process of experimenting with these new responses to see if the outcome is better, worse, or the same. The goal is for teachers to feel more empowered with more tools in their box.

Teaching these skills over time is how schools can help students be leaders of themselves and their families, schools, and communities. Students are in desperate need of this type of learning, at all grade levels. I hope this book begins a conversation about Brave Teaching, and I look forward to hearing about the results.

ACKNOWLEDGMENTS

KRISSY WRITES: First and foremost, I want to express my deep appreciation to Sarah Love. Through her unique quest to increase her son's emotional resilience, she found my book *Brave Parenting*, and artfully applied it to both her home and classroom. Her continued quest to bring this perspective to all teachers led to the project to write this book. Thank you, Sarah, for your commitment to this book and your dedication to all teachers.

I would also like to thank all parents who, like Sarah, have read my books. Hearing your stories about how after applying the concepts from my books you reached new outcomes in your parent–child relationship is what keeps me going.

As Sarah and I began to write this book, it felt like we were tapping into a huge unmet need, as parents, teachers, school-board members, and other educators were asking for early versions of the book to bring to their schools and classrooms—ASAP! There is a skills gap between school curriculums and students' emotional resiliency to do the academic work. Through *Brave Teaching* and increased emotional attunement to students, we hope to close this gap. I want to thank all the individuals who showed interested and encouraged this project.

My friend and girls advocate Hillery Maxymillian and school-board member Neal Maxymillian gave me feedback on an early version of this manuscript. Thanks, Hill and Neal: you both have keen eyes and good insights!

I'd like to thank my family and friends for believing in me, knowing I have more books to write, and encouraging me to keep reaching new audiences. Thank you to Martin Rowe at Lantern Books for believing in the book and recognizing its important contribution.

❧ **SARAH WRITES**: Thank you to all the teachers at Black Forest Hills Elementary for being willing to listen and trying out pieces from this book!

To Krissy: Thank you for taking a risk with me, and giving me the opportunity to write with you. Your knowledge and expertise have forever changed my parenting as well as my teaching career.

To Mom, Dad, and Sister: Thanks for always supporting my strong-willed personality. I took the risk because of you guys.

To my fabulous son, Logan, and beautiful step-daughter, Piper: Thank you for challenging me as a mom every day and showing me what unconditional love is.

To my partner, Jeff: Thank you for the unconditional support to follow my dreams. ❧

GLOSSARY

Accountability Measures: Actions used to hold someone accountable for an unhealthy or inappropriate choice. Also called a consequence.

Behavioral Boundaries: The identification of what behavior is acceptable or unacceptable.

Choices: Giving options. Choices diffuse control and disrupt power struggles.

Collaborative Group Problem-Solving: Asking students to solve the problem as a group, without adults guiding them to an answer.

Delayed Gratification: An ability to work hard and complete a task without an instant reward.

Emotional Attunement: Sensitive response to the emotions of others; being on someone's emotional wavelength.

Enmeshment: When a parent or adult is overly involved with a child's feelings, behaviors, or problems and tries to fix or change them to feel better about themselves.

Executive Functioning: The cognitive ability to understand and respond to internal emotional states and external stressors such that personal and social behavior is appropriate and proportionate.

Feelings Checks: Taking a few moments to survey our emotional landscape to identify a feeling word that matches our current state.

Four Essential Ingredients: These are emotional attunement, behavioral boundaries, safety, and valuing struggle. All four, based on wilderness therapy, promote maturation.

Growth Mindset: An orientation toward seeing challenges around learning as a means of growing in knowledge, skills, and maturity.

Helicopter Parenting: A contemporary phrase to describe parents who "hover" over their children's lives, taking control of all of their activities.

Internal Skill: Ability to cope with stress, adversity, or discomfort without relying on external support or actions.

Learning Container: The space where maturation, internal skill-development, and emotional resilience takes place.

Maturation: An ability in children to accept their external reality and learn to self-manage their internal reality.

Mirroring: A form of attentiveness and responsiveness where the listener reflects (either visibly or audibly) a recognition or understanding of the speaker's emotional state or wishes.

Problem-solve: An ability to recognize there is a problem, comprehend its nature, seek a solution, and then apply those skills to similar problems (whether in math or in life).

Safety: A situation where an adult is in charge and creates security and order.

Self-Regulation: The ability for someone to be self-aware and identify his or her emotions, to own that feeling, and then to control their subsequent behavior.

Teacher Authority: The ability of a teacher to establish order and discipline in a classroom and encourage engaged and self-directed learning among students.

ABOUT THE AUTHORS

Photo: Shamus McKim

KRISSY POZATEK, MSW, is a former wilderness therapist and current parent coach. It is her quest to bring the internal-resiliency skills that kids gain from the wilderness into everyday parenting. She is the author of *Brave Parenting* and *The Parallel Process*. In addition to parent-coaching and writing, Krissy is a public speaker and conducts parent workshops and seminars nationally. Krissy was also a visiting professor at her alma matter, Middlebury College, Vermont.

Photo: Sarah Love

SARAH LOVE is an elementary-school teacher in the Cherry Creek School District in Aurora, Colorado. Inspired by her desire to help people, she knew she wanted to be an educator early on in her life. She graduated from Metropolitan State College with a bachelor's degree in behavioral science and subsequently a master's degree in special education from Colorado University–Denver. She has been a teacher for twelve years in multiple grades. She has served as a behavior specialist throughout her career. Intrigued by the science of social and emotional behaviors, she has channeled this passion into her first book with Krissy.

ABOUT THE PUBLISHER

LANTERN BOOKS was founded in 1999 on the principle of living with a greater depth and commitment to the preservation of the natural world. In addition to publishing books on animal advocacy, vegetarianism, religion, and environmentalism, Lantern is dedicated to printing books in the United States on recycled paper and saving resources in day-to-day operations. Lantern is honored to be a recipient of the highest standard in environmentally responsible publishing from the Green Press Initiative.

lanternbooks.com